AUTOMATIC AMBITION:

The Guide to Having a Champion's Mindset

Reemus Boxing

Publisher: Independent Publishing Network

Company: Reemus Boxing

Email: Reemus@reemusboxing.com

Please direct all enquiries to the author

ISBN 9781789269048

London, United Kingdom

www.ReemusBoxing.com

TABLE OF CONTENTS

INTRODUCTION

The Champion's Mindset, AKA 'Champ-Set'

I hate the introduction part. I really do. Usually, I find it to be the most boring chapter of the book—yet very important. The introduction makes it so much easier to understand the whole book. Don't skip; I'll be quick...

Every day, millions of fighters around the world work themselves to death in an effort to achieve the dreams of their career one day. However, the cold truth is that a great majority of them will fail. It is just the truth. For a boxer, failure is more painful than for the average person. Fighters risk their health, wealth, life, and comfort to get to the top of this sport. Failing in this sport will not be worth the cost of your effort.

The popular belief is that the champions of tomorrow are the fighters that are naturally talented or simply just blessed by God. Wrong. I have hope for you. You have a much greater control over your destiny than that, don't you think?

There have been plenty of fighters, like the ones in this book, who didn't have it easy, and had to fight for their dream. They had to *make* it happen if they wanted to sit down on the golden throne. *You* can make it, no matter the circumstances, and you need to know it on a subconscious level. Because once you believe it, it won't be long before you achieve it.

This is what makes a winner. It is a champion's mindset, or what I call 'Champ-set' for short, that makes people great. Champ-set is the winner's state of mind. You can only become a champion if you have a champion's mindset. And having a champion's mindset is not a place or a temporary title. But, unfortunately, those failing fighters have no idea that a winning mentality is what actually gets the belt.

Once you have been exposed to the truth of success, you can't turn back. You look at the world differently, and instead of being unsure about whether you can make it or not, you then start to believe in the dream.

That's the reason for which this book is made: for the fighter with a dream. With this book, I want to provide you with the tools to make it a reality. Those tools can be found by looking at the past champions.

Each chapter centres on one particular icon. The first half of the book focuses on building up that belief and crafting your vision with a champion's mindset. To do this, there are **action affirmations** or **action visualisations** for you throughout the chapters.

An affirmation is simply a statement said with strong faith that empowers you to achieve your desired goals. When you do affirmations, you are declaring that statement as being true for you. The affirmations in this book are the mantras of a champion. This mental technique works splendidly to transform you from a fighter who has limiting beliefs to a champion who is free of the doubts that stop him from performing at the highest level.

Affirmations create a good feeling within yourself, providing the platform to build strong belief upon. You must work on the affirmations every day. Repeat them throughout the week to bombard the negative thoughts that are present in your mind and replace them with positive ones.

Try to focus on set affirmations from each chapter on each specific day. I suggest that you take a few minutes in the early morning and late at night to repeat your affirmations. It can be said either out loud or in your head. If said out loud, repeat in a low voice and at least ten times generally.

The **visualisation** techniques work with the affirmations to impact your subconscious mind. A visualisation requires you to close your eyes and vividly picture yourself achieving your desired goals. A visualisation is a visual representation of an affirmation, and it helps to impact both the subconscious and conscious mind in a powerful way.

Once you can see yourself in the act, achieving something, you become more confident in bringing this to reality. You will begin to draw in the people, resources, and results that you want, because your focus will be dictated by what you are visualising.

You will begin to pinpoint the methods and tools you need in order to attain the image you have in your mind. With increased belief, you will have a higher level of motivation to achieve the dreams you want.

Similar to affirmations, I would suggest you do it when you wake up and before you sleep, and in daily moments when you are still (on train journeys, waiting in the barber's, waiting in line, etc.). Also, before and after your training sessions are particularly good times. It works best if you can sit or lay down, close your eyes, and breathe in and out slowly for about a minute or 6-8 times. Once relaxed, you can place powerful imagery in your mind.

The general methods of visualisation for this book include you watching yourself from a camera's perspective, as if you have your own reality show. Imagine you are in a movie theatre, watching yourself on a big screen. Also, at other times, when you must deepen the experience, or focus on the environment around you, take the perspective from your own point of view, through your eye's view. There will also be other specific mental exercises to follow.

To successfully visualise, you must be as vivid and specific as you can, when placing the image in your mind, down to the clothing, facial expressions, and details of the environment.

Sugar Ray Leonard would even sensualise it, meaning he added his senses to the imagery. Likewise, you should add the details of the physical feelings, the taste or smells, and the sounds that could be in the scene. Try to experience the emotion of a visualisation too. This helps to impact you even more powerfully. You must know this so you can personalise the set routines provided, which makes the visualisation more effective.

Next, the second half of the book helps you project your vision into the world. In this section, there are practical steps you must implement. These **assignments** help you to actively get the results that you want. The tasks vary in the amount of time and effort required to complete.

It is good to read, but you must also act on what you learn, or it will not be of any worth. The assignments actively force your dream to take form. They will help you to decide how to generally go about making decisions in your career to progress your training, all based on what a champion would do.

If you are a boxing coach, then consider the initial boost of doing an affirmation, visualisation or assignment for your fighter. Tell your fighter, 'You are a champion', and they will start to believe and say it themselves. Sit them down and guide them through a visualisation of them holding the championship belt. Most coaches won't excel in this area. This is where you will separate yourself from the competition.

And if you are not a fighter or even an athlete, you can still benefit from this book. You will just need to tweak and customise the principles that are explained so it fits the craft you are in. Whether you are a 100m sprinter, an entrepreneur, a musician or a journalist, it does not matter. Read the book through the lens of your personal world and adjust the advice to your needs. Customise the affirmations, visualisation exercises, and assignments, according to your specific niche.

It isn't enough to learn and admire the champions of before. We must act so we can share some of the glory. Let's go, champ!

Disclaimer: The time of writing for this book is late 2018. The chapters focus on specific champions from both the present and the past. In the volatile sport of boxing, endless victories are a rarity. The legendary Muhummad Ali lost five times. But despite this, he is still 'The Greatest of all Time'. It is real possibility that one of the current fighters (who are unbeaten) in the book will suffer a loss sooner or later. It's important to understand that if, or when, that happens, it does not diminish your respect of their achievements up until that point. The principles that got them to that point are still valid and will help you as you try to add accomplishments to your résumé.

PART 1: CRAFT THE VISION

THE DREAM BEGINS IN YOU

'Sugar' Ray Leonard: Winning Against the Odds

One of the sport's most memorable moments came on 6 April 1987 in the modern mecca of boxing, Las Vegas. In Caesar's Palace, 'Sugar' Ray Leonard (36-3-1, 25KO) attempted a feat that by all standards of logic was considered delusional, just as much as it seemed suicidal.

Ray Leonard was attempting to relieve the intimidating figure of Marvin Hagler of his throne. A year earlier, in 1986, the middleweight champion, Marvin Hagler, took on tough challenger John Mugabi. After a spirited rally from the challenger, Hagler broke down Mugabi and knocked him out in typical relentless fashion.

Ray was in attendance that night, sitting ringside with actor Michael J. Fox. After seemingly spotting a chink in Hagler's performance, he leaned over and said, 'Michael, I can beat this guy,' to which Michael replied, 'Sure you can, Ray. Do you want another beer?'

The apparent delusion of the task wasn't only down to the fact that Hagler had pulverised every opponent he had previously faced for the last five years. But that in those five years, Leonard had only fought once due to a detached retina, winning a lacklustre victory against journeyman Kevin Howard. How could he topple the ferociously on-form Hagler?

After that Hagler-Mugabi match, Leonard called his manager, Mike Trainer, at 2 a.m. that same night, requesting to make the fight. 'Ray, have you been drinking?' Mike instantly asked. 'Yes. But that's not the point. I can beat him,' Ray replied. He seemed to be the only person that believed it.

Despite Sugar Ray's previous dominance in the welterweight and junior middleweight divisions, most pundits agreed that moving up in weight class forfeited any hope of being the favourite. Prior to the bout, a 67-man poll had 60 reporters who predicted that Hagler would be the winner, and 52 of them expected it to be a knockout win for the champion. Many of those reporters were even friends of Leonard's.

Leonard's family also shared the feeling. They thought Ray was crazy for even considering the match. 'Who is your tune-up?' his brother Derrik asked. 'Hagler,' Ray replied. 'No, I said who is your *tune-up?*' Derrik insisted, as if Leonard couldn't have heard him correctly. 'Hagler' was the answer he received again.

From friends, like boxing commentator Howard Cosell, to family, like wife Juanita, no one could see the sanity in Ray's pursuit. Ray was risking his career legacy as well as his health. But the more Ray thought about it, the more he believed he could do it.

Ray's belief drove him to train with outrageous dedication. He brought in top-quality sparring partners, one being Quincy Taylor, a future world champion. He sparred more than 200 rounds and was diligent with his roadwork and gym-work.

Come the night of the fight, his body mirrored the figure of Spartacus. And Ray believed that as long as his mind was right like when he faced Hearns and Duran, where the only thing that mattered in life was winning, once he got there, nothing could stop him. He believed it, and that's all that mattered.

On that Las Vegas night, Leonard proved all his doubters wrong, performing magnificently in a tough 12-round battle with the champion. It was a back and forth contest, with Ray fighting as the beautiful 'pure boxer'. His efforts secured him a split decision victory, and he became the new middleweight champion. It was the greatest feat of his career, considering the circumstances (of inactivity and Hagler's dominance). He had overcome not just the champion, but the mental challenges that came along with the match.

Ray's stubborn belief in his own potential sets the standard for believing in your own ability. When others don't believe, you must. When others don't see it in you, you must. You must believe in yourself or give up the ability to access your deepest potential.

The Power of the Mind

There is one particular weapon which will determine your ability to form a champion's mindset. It ignites your inner greatness, and it is a trait that all the elite boxing champions share together. Without it, it will be impossible for you to join that illustrious list of champions.

The special trait is belief. You must have belief in your boxing goals and truly know that they are in your reach. It isn't enough to think that becoming a great champion is perhaps potentially possible. You must truly feel on the deepest level that it can be a realistic expectation for you.

'Sugar' Ray Leonard exhibited this same level of belief as a youngster. Before he had any claim to fame, and whilst an amateur, he would run to school behind the school bus to intensify his training. As you could imagine, his schoolmates thought he was crazy. But the young Ray believed his hard work would pay off in a few years. Long before his success, he made the decision to believe in the dream.

Belief doesn't directly get you the results you want; your actions do. These 'actions' refer to your training in the gym and performance in the ring. But belief is important because, without it, you will struggle to take action in the right way. A winner is someone who is consistently taking action in a way that will lead to his victory and progress. In other words, he trains right, and he fights at a high level.

Consistency is vital if you wish to be a champion, and it is something that cannot be faked. It is hard to win often if you aren't really deserving of it. So, you must have belief ingrained into you so that it becomes natural to take the right action frequently and attract winning results regularly. To achieve this state of winning consistency, you need a positive mindset that drives the belief that makes it possible. And to acquire this mindset, you must control your inner dialogue and self-attitude.

What do you say to yourself about yourself and what do you feel on a daily basis? This is your 'inner reality'. It is your everyday thoughts and feelings about yourself and the world around you. It affects what you are able to do and how you do it. Your inner vision unlocks the ability to do what needs to be done so you can later become a champion.

In the words of 'Sugar' Ray Leonard's hero Muhammad Ali, 'right now you are becoming, what you are thinking.' So, what are you thinking right now about yourself and your career?

Many fighters do not have any idea that how they talk to themselves is affecting their ability to perform in the ring and the gym. And the few that do, they still struggle to fine-tune their thinking patterns to that of a champion's mindset.

Making it worse, there are very few places or people to go to if you want to work on your mindset. For example, when was the last time your trainer stressed the importance of believing that you are worthy of winning multiple championships? And I mean *really* stressed on improving your mind.

Do trainers do this with the same intensity they stress you should work out? It is rare. Most trainers themselves don't know how to instil this belief in fighters. They are totally oblivious to its importance. There are many trainers but few motivational teachers.

MAKING THE CHANGE RIGHT NOW

Sow the Seeds of a Champion

All your thoughts must be drenched with positivity and potential. You must wake up in the morning with positive explanations about why you are waking up early to run. You must walk to the boxing gym with positive affirmations running through your mind. And in times of frustration, you must stay positive about how you can turn adversities into your advantage.

The only way you can start to think like a champ is to decide first that you are going to make the effort to change your thoughts. You must make the decision right now, no matter where you are at, that you are a champion. This must be done with the clear intention of knowing it will benefit your career.

Even without the belt, you must decide that an inner champion is already in you, so we can simply work on bringing it out. The question is, will you do what is needed to bring this quality to the surface? Without making that decision, it will be impossible. Decide *right now* that you will do what it takes to get this mindset. Only when you have made that decision, the real journey starts.

In 1972, the 16-year-old Ray Leonard failed to make the Olympic team of that year. He was upset about it, but the coach told him not to worry, 'I'm sure you'll make the next Olympics.' This was true, and Leonard was much better prepared for the 1976 Olympics, and he did end up winning the gold medal four years later. Despite the setback in '72, Ray didn't lose belief. He had made the decision, and he knew he was a champion even when he had lost; it was only a matter of time before he could let it out.

Champ Affirmations:

Statements that ignite Champ-set.

'I'm a champion. I have the belt, and I passionately believe I'm an elite fighter.'

'I am one of the greatest fighters in the world; I can beat the best fighters in my division.'

'I am a winner, and I can achieve anything I desire.'

Access a Champion's Inner Power

If your mind doesn't believe it can do something, then you will not be able to do it. The results of a winner are exclusive to the person who acts like one. And the actions of a winner are exclusive to the type of person who believes that he is one.

Alternatively, a fighter with a loser's mentality doesn't have access to the abilities of a winner. This is what separates the naturally talented good from the ambitious greats who worked hard. It isn't just their natural talents; talented fighters must also believe that they are worth the championship. The physical qualities are only a by-product of the most important aspect: their psychology.

Fortunately, it is possible to grow Champ-set. You can do this by changing your inner reality. Adjust the daily affirmations you say to yourself and the perception you have of yourself. This can be done instantly.

It is easy for you to tell yourself good things about yourself. It is simple to say something along the lines of 'I can be the greatest boxer that ever came out of my city,' even if this still seems like a fantasy. The hard part is making it happen before impatience starts to set in.

After, comes the most important part: action. The objective of improving your mind is to train and fight effectively. Once you sort out the mental side, it becomes easy to do this; you place yourself in a cycle of positivity and fearless executing, until it becomes natural and repetitive. This cycle takes time to gain momentum, before you reap its rewards, but if you desire to be a magnificent champion, patience will be a small cost.

Let's take a moment to reflect with raw honesty. If we were to make a list of your activities over the last week, would it reflect the routine of a future legend? Stop and ask yourself, have you been working as hard as you could have? And I don't mean harder than everyone in your gym; I mean the absolute hardest that you can.

Imagine a camera had followed you for the last week. If that footage were to be put out today, would it be an inspirational documentary, showing you work hard like a champion is supposed to? Would it show how ambitious you are? Take a moment to assess your daily actions.

Is success your *highest* priority? Is the work you are putting in worthy of winning the championship? Most likely, there is room for improvement. But don't beat yourself up if you feel that you have been slacking. Just make a change. Let's do the things that a champion would do.

Champ Visualisation: the 'Day in the Life of a Champion' Exercise

In the morning, imagine how well your day is going to go. Envision going through your day like a champion would. Imagine that you have a championship fight at the end of the week. See yourself being followed by a cameraman from a major TV outlet, like HBO. Visualise getting out of bed and ready to run in the morning with the cameraman following your every move.

Imagine the camera following you as you do your daily activities. Imagine walking and preparing with the body language of a confident champion, interacting with people who are in admiration of your ability.

As you see yourself attending your training sessions, imagine there are cameras around you and raving fans trying to get a glimpse of the champion. After that training session, see yourself speaking into the camera, letting your fans know how confident you are of winning. For the closing scene, close the door on the camera, giving the camera a confident wink before you head to bed.

Why Can't It Be You?

If other fighters have done enough before to secure a place in history, why can't you too? It may seem mythical at this point. But the greats from the past are human, just like you. They had to follow the process and work hard. Only after putting in the work, did they grow into amazing champions.

If you do the same thing and go through the same process, you will get the same results. Even if you don't see your dream as realistic right now, be bold and just believe for now. It will start to become more realistic as time goes on. Strive to act as the champion you wish to become, and it will happen.

Back in Ray's amateur days, he invited his parents to his first match so they could see him fight for the first time. His parents saw him as a soft kid and certainly didn't take him seriously as a practitioner of violence. 'You can't fight,' was the initial reply his father gave upon hearing that he was actually going through with it.

After Ray Leonard had started to win some early fights in the amateurs, his father began to believe in his potential. He was now a believer and excitedly raved about his son to friends. Even though Ray had been doing well, they said, 'Your son is too small, he will never be anything in boxing,' to which his father replied, 'He will; you just wait.'

Ray turned out to be quite something in the sport of boxing. He won titles in five different weight classes and was the first boxer to earn more than one hundred million dollars in fight purses. But before he had shown the world his ability, no one else could see it. With progress and time, those doubters turned into believers. It takes work, but achieving your dream can be done.

Champ Assignment: the 30/60 Promise

Promise that you will be open-minded. Even if you do not initially agree with the possibilities just yet, try to accept that it could be true. Really commit to executing the suggestions in this practical guide for the next 30 days. Once you see benefits, use this as motivation to commit for another 60 days. If you truly commit, you will gain Champ-Set in the next 3 months.

BELIEF MAKES CHAMPIONS

Deontay Wilder: See Success And Eliminate Doubts

'Don't worry about what you can't do. Focus on what you will do. If you believe in yourself, if you say you gon' do something, if you believe you're the best in here, then you ain't gonna have no doubts. You ain't gon' say "what if?" or "I hope to do this" or "I hope to do what I say was gonna do, "what if I don't do it?", "what if I don't knock him out?" When I say things, I don't have a shadow of doubt. I believe a thousand percent in what I say.'

Deontay Wilder

From 2015, one of the Heavyweight thrones was occupied by a fighter who very few could comprehend how his wild style managed to destroy every challenger he faced. This fighter is Deontay Wilder (40-0-1, 39KO) of Alabama. The WBC king stands as an amazing physical specimen with a right-hand punch that would intimidate Hercules.

Up until 2018 (at the time of writing), he has knocked out every single fighter he has ever faced, besides a draw with Tyson Fury. He has defended his title numerous times, after winning it from Bermane Stiverne. However, his critics argued that his style lacks technical finesse, as he swings wildly and often throws himself off balance.

Still, he gets the job done. In almost every single fight he's been in thus far, there lies a sequence of blows that would make the boxing purists choke. Wilder swings as wild as the crazy kid in the school playground. It's a style that shouldn't work, but it's one that worked for him.

The only thing that enables such an unorthodox style to work in such a devastating fashion is his belief that it should work. If Deontay didn't believe it would work, it wouldn't. By intensely believing that he can defeat his opponent in his own way, he trains and progresses in accordance with this thought.

Not only has he won fights, but he brutally sent his opponents into deep unconsciousness. Whenever he stepped into the ring, Deontay believed that the outcome would be victory, no matter the style he has. With this set in his mind, every action that followed was to make that vision a reality. Any other thought about anything else is a waste of a fighter's energy.

'If I say I'ma do something, it ain't gonna be like "damn what if I don't do it?" I don't worry about that. I worry about what I said, and I'm gon' do it,' says Wilder. You must focus on forging great self-belief. You will start to grow the ability to make those beliefs come true, and you will not give an ounce of energy to the doubts that stop you from turning those beliefs into reality.

You Can't Do More Than the Level of Your Belief

When a boxer wins one fight in a great manner, we call the performance great. But when that same fighter performs great ten times, we call the *fighter* great. Belief will win you matches consistently, and consistency is what makes a fighter great.

One-off performances that are great could be down to luck or chance. But if you can consistently perform at a high level, you prove that the determining factor is you, and not a lucky fluke. This is the level at which you must aspire to be; belief is the weapon you need to reach it.

Belief, or lack of it, determines what you are able to do in the ring and the gym. Belief is what allows you to go through the pain and frustration in training to bring yourself up to the level you want. Belief is prerequisite for becoming who you want to become. It is the thing that helps you get there.

With self-belief, you will practise until you eventually master what you feel you should be able to do. For example, if you do not believe you have it in you to win world titles and make history, it will be impossible for you to go through the trouble of attempting it. Even if you do not have much confidence at this exact moment, you need to first use your imagination to open your mind up.

Your potential is like a seed of a tree. In this seed, lies a tree, which has simply not grown. Your belief is like the healthy nutrient that is needed to feed the seed, so the seed grows into what it already is.

Alternatively, fear and self-limitations are like poisons, which will transform your seed into a negative weed. Believing in your fears will lead to doubts. With a fearful mind, it is difficult to unleash your vision. Manage your beliefs and watch what you feed your mind. Do you feed your mind with healthy doses of belief or poisonous doses of doubts?

The unorthodox Wilder credits much of his success to his use of visualisation; it helps to 'strengthen my mind,' as he says. Before even being in the ring, he visualises fighting his opponent to the point that he has 'fought him 100 times, and he doesn't even know it,' by the time fight night comes.

However, even more practically, it helps him to create and search for strategies to achieve that visualised scene. You must also take the same approach. This will encourage you to get into perfect condition, as you feed the champion within you.

FIGHT THE NAYSAYERS

The Outside Farmers of Weeds

One of the dangers that we face is that the weeds of fear and doubt may be planted by others. Naturally, we learn from other people how to act and think. If those around us are innovative, positive and like to encourage, then this is truly special. A fighter who can take in knowledge in this way can learn much quicker than his peers. However, the problem is that it is just as easy to soak up bad thoughts if those around us think negatively.

If you are not surrounded by people that see much potential in themselves, it is likely that they will project that same lack of belief onto you. Can you see the problem here? In our sport, which is one of the most dangerous of all, it is much easier for people to talk about the dangers we face and the risks in the ring. While this is a reality, if that same person doesn't talk about the great rewards that you could also reap from the sport, then this means they are biased.

Separating yourself from other people's doubts is extremely important to become a champion. As you advance, you will need to prevent yourself from ingraining the negative vibes from people who do not believe in success.

Champ Affirmations:

These affirmations are focused on current challenges.

In the dressing room before a fight: 'I have already defeated my opponent; I have no doubt in my mind about what I can do.'

Before a training session: 'I am getting into superb condition, and I have the fitness of a gladiator.'

Before a sparring session: 'I am going to perform supremely. I was made for success.'

The Negative Fake Experts

'How can anyone else say anything about boxing if you've never experienced it? Do you know what it feels like to walk that tunnel?'

- Deontay Wilder

Fighters must resist the influence of people with no experience in the sport. Usually, their negative criticism comes from insecurity and lacks practicality. This hurts you more than it helps. As Wilder says, 'People say a lot of things. How can anybody else say anything about boxing if you've never experienced it? Do you know what it's like to walk that tunnel (to the ring)? How do you know what it takes to be a champion?' Most people do not, but they will downplay a fighter's ambition as if they have the experience to judge.

This type of criticism is called 'fake expertise', and it can limit the dreams of a fighter. A 'fake expert' is a person who comments on an experience as if he or she knows what will happen, without actually having any such experience to justify this comment. Their 'knowledge' is only based on opinion, and they are usually biased.

Furthermore, they often strongly believe in their opinion about a subject and are determined to make others believe it too. This can become a problem only when a fighter allows fake experts with a negative mindset to influence his actions.

In sports, especially in boxing, there are more failures than successes. This is especially the case on the way to the top. But this is what makes success so attractive. It is impressive to become a champion because most cannot achieve it. You are one of the few, when you reach the top.

For every one champion, there are a few million boxers who will never become one. And for every victory you accomplish, there were literally hundreds of painful failures you have to endure to get there. Most people want to entirely avoid those failures, and this is reflected in the advice given to fighters.

Negative fake experts use limiting language when describing your chances of success, focusing on trying to discourage you. For example, imagine you are thinking about making a major career change. This change could include wanting to move to a bigger city where there are more opportunities or better coaches.

This decision must be made logically, and you must weigh up *both* the pros and cons. However, a negative fake expert with a limited mindset will automatically shut down the pros and focus solely on the cons. They will only focus on the potential negative outcome, even if there is just as much of a reason to predict a positive outcome. A negative fake expert will talk you out of it. Rather than encouraging, fake experts discourage.

On the other hand, it isn't just other people that do it to us, but many times, we do it to ourselves. In some cases, an outsider may actually encourage you to try a new challenge. And *you* can be the negative fake expert yourself. You may quickly say, 'No, I can't do that' or 'Maybe it's easy for you, but for me, I couldn't do that,' before you have even tried it. If you do this more than once, you will start to make a habit out of talking down to yourself.

How do you fix it? The remedy is to judge *only* on experience. Never assume and always just try before you judge. Let experience dictate if your claim is true. Gaining experience will increase your confidence, as you learn what you are able to do. Take on the challenge and try. After gaining experience, your knowledge will be based on *evidence*.

This also means that if you need advice, then it is best to get it from someone who has gone through the experience themselves successfully. An experienced person cannot replace the value of personal experience, but they are the closest thing to it. They will let you know the truth, without being biased like the average fake expert.

If you take anything from this book, let it be this. This issue is so important because it is one of the hardest things for fighters to spot. And it is one of the major reasons why many boxers never reach their potential. They limit themselves before they ever truly try.

Champ Visualisation: 'Your Favourite Fighter' Exercise

Imagine taking on a challenge and your favourite fighter is by your side. Deontay Wilder will be the example in this exercise.

At the gym: when warming up, imagine Wilder to your left doing it with you. Envision a friend of yours at the front of the room, holding up your championship belt. Once you start hitting the heavy bag, Wilder is sharing it with you, throwing punches on the other side. Imagine Wilder increasing the intensity of his punches on his heavy bag. Respond to this by increasing the intensity of your punches too.

When you are on the speed bag, imagine Wilder on the other side, telling you to keep going. When you are skipping, look over to the side and see Wilder skipping as well. When you are sparring in between rounds, Wilder is standing at the ropes cheering you on.

On runs: when running, imagine Wilder jogging by your side. Be inspired by a champion being at your side and raise your standard to that of an elite fighter's. Maintain a fast pace when you start to tire, and don't let Wilder outrun you. On the last half mile, speed up and increase the pace for the last leg. Try to outrun the champion.

'I always tell people if you speak it, believe it, receive it, then you shall do that. And I speak things because I want to be a living

witness. It's nothing like showing people, then they believe it. Because a lot of people always say I have to see it to believe it. If that's the case, then I show people each and every time that ima show you [first], and you'll believe in it.'

Deontay Wilder

THE KING OF YOUR WORLD

Conor McGregor: Control Your Self-Belief

'You have to think something, so why not think you're the best to ever do it? Why not think of yourself as a king?'

Conor McGregor

Long before Irishman Conor McGregor (21-4, 18KO/1SUB) became a multiple world champion in MMA, he always believed that he not only had the potential to be great, but that he was *already* great. He proved that he's a great UFC (Ultimate Fighting Championship) fighter, becoming the first fighter to hold two divisional world titles at the same time in the UFC, and later challenged the legendary Floyd Mayweather Jr in a record-breaking billion-dollar match in his very first official boxing match.

McGregor earned respect as a great champion due to the massive success he attained. But more important for you is to know that before McGregor etched out this earned impression, long before anyone else believed in him, when no one did, he believed in himself.

Asked if he could have envisioned himself in such a successful position when he was younger, McGregor replied to reporters, 'I had to envision it, because if I didn't, I wouldn't be here. So not only did I envision it, I envisioned it so much that, so clearly and so precisely in my head, that I am here now.'

Growing up, McGregor had no ounce of success in the world around him to take inspiration from. Many people in this position would struggle to find any reason to be inspired from within. Conor came from nothing and could safely be described as a bum to the naked eye. He would often hang out with the wrong crowd as a youngster and was totally distracted from any ambitious goal.

Conor found himself ushered into a plumbing apprenticeship, simply because, according to his words, 'that's what culture told me I must do.' However, he quit 18 months later to the great dismay of his angered father. But Conor fought back and rejected his father's demands to go back. He was on welfare and had no life prospects, but despite the lowly position he was in, Conor always knew he was a winner deep inside.

He never let his outer environment define whether he was great or not; he simply thought about himself, as *he* wanted to think of himself, not what society, family, or friends thought of him. When his father tried to force him to return to the plumbing apprenticeship, he firmly rejected, which led to furious fights between the two. This stubbornness later paid off as he poured his all into combat sports soon after and shot to stardom in a few years.

Staying grounded in your self-belief drives a fighter to excel in his sport. You must be willing and wanting to view yourself as the champ, even before you have the belt. You must believe you are already a champion so much, that it makes no sense that you are not training your ass off trying to attain what you already believe is yours. Like Conor, you must do this against the resistance of the world telling you that you are not what you think you are.

From rising through the ranks of the UFC, up to the mega-bout with Mayweather, Conor had encountered intense doubt from critics at every challenge. But at every step, he outperformed their expectations. You must be the same. Do not limit your belief of who you are and what you can do to people's expectation. Set it yourself.

Create Your Own World

Your self-perception strongly affects your ability to unlock self-belief. Though the world is the same, we all view it differently. Your thoughts and beliefs are *your own* truth. The way you see things is unique, and all of what you do, believe, and feel comes from that unique perception that only you have. *You* create your own reality. Your perspective on the world is down to you. More importantly, your perspective on *yourself* is also down to you.

Take the example of debating with another fight fan on the greatest fighter in history. When you speak about who you believe is the greatest, your answer will be based on your own unique reasoning. Even if someone disagrees with you, you will stand by your own belief, no matter what they say. However, when it comes down to it, there is no right or wrong answer; it is all down to personal opinion. Even as I say this, you probably still stand by your opinion of who is the best, as if it is a fact.

Now, imagine if you could take that same level of stubbornness in who is the greatest … and apply it to yourself? It may seem illogical to look at yourself as the future's greatest fighter. But why not? Any perception of who is the best fighter isn't really a fact anyway. So, if you're going to have an opinion on who is the greatest, why not have this opinion of yourself? This is better than committing that same energy to another person.

Like McGregor did, you can stake a claim to the number one spot right now. It is the only way it will eventually happen. No one is inherently 'just better' than you. We see fighters like McGregor speak loud with confidence and draw people to them charismatically. We may tell ourselves that these people are just blessed by God (and maybe on some level they are) but it still doesn't justify why you should not believe in yourself with the same level of intensity.

LEAD YOUR OWN MIND

You Have to Think Something. Why Not Think You're Great?

'If you see yourself as the king, if you see yourself with all the belts and everything, no matter what no one else says, as long as you see that, and really believe in it, then that's what's going to

happen ... Who says what way you see things? Who says what you see yourself as?'

Conor McGregor

It is up to you whether you think positively or negatively. What is certain, though, is that you have no choice but to think one of the two. Since this is the case, you may as well pick the best option: think positively. Whichever statement you make about your chances, you aren't wrong.

Pick the one which is more beneficial to you. Even if you failed in your quest to be a multi-division world champion, you would most likely still be a boxing show headliner or a world-title challenger at the very least. Reach for the stars and you might land on the moon.' But reach for the moon and you might only get the clouds. Nothing is in the clouds.

If you do not make the effort to think positively, you will let doubts creep in. That does not help your long-term goals, so you must reject the negative thinking. For your sake, choose to believe in the winning side. Once you set up your life to automate this positive thinking, it will become effortless.

Long before Conor McGregor beat Jose Aldo for the world featherweight title in thirteen seconds, was he the champion? To the world, he wasn't, but to *himself*, he was. Technically, he wasn't, but he chose to believe in that dream. He made it up in his head, but by strongly believing in it, it came true.

Before he claimed the lightweight title, when he defeated Eddie Alvarez, was he the lightweight champion? On paper, he wasn't, but to *himself*, he was. Before he beat his nemesis Nate Diaz in the rematch, had he beaten Nate Diaz? To the critics, he hadn't, but to *himself*, he had. You must feel and truly believe that history has already written your success, and it is only a matter of time to live out the script.

One of the issues we face when trying to state our plan is the fears of other people's opinions. We care about other people's judgement. The infection of the negative fake expertise is widespread. It is easy to downgrade your ambitions to small dreams, because you know others won't believe in it. Rather than saying 'I can be a multidivisional world champion,' you might be timid and say, 'I just want to try and headline a show,' in front of other people. Fight it.

What Will You Become?

'I love this stuff. This is what gives me energy, putting it out there for the world to see. And then going out and doing it. There's no better feeling in the world than that. And it's as easy as that: say what you're gonna do, then do it.'

Conor McGregor

To create a prophecy for yourself, you must establish what it is that you want to become in the ring. You must have a very clear vision of the type of champion you wish to be. What traits do you want to possess? How would you like to operate in the ring? How would you like the fans to see your style? You have to specifically define the characteristics you want to have when fighting.

More than just envisioning the fighter you want to be in the ring, you can also paint a vision of what the future will look like out of the ring. What specific successes do you want to attain? What accomplishments do you want to achieve? By what year could you realistically do it? Are you doing it for your family, or do you want to inspire your country?

You can never be too specific when it comes to defining your future. The plan will evolve as time goes by and you gain new experience. It's crazy that we are rarely taught to plan our careers, but this is a necessity for a champion-in-training. How can we expect to achieve it, if we don't see it and create the path?

Champ Assignment: Making the Prophecy

Physically write down, either on a paper or on your phone, three to five of the main goals that you want to achieve in your career. Write it in chronological order. In bullet points below each goal, add details. Add the inspiration that drives you, the expected year it can be done, why few people have done it, and why you are one that can complete the task.

Champ Visualisation: the 'Goal TV' Exercise

You've written the script; now see the prophecy being done in your mind.

Imagine a wide field. In this green space, there is a bright white building. Imagine you are walking up to the door of this building, and you see the words 'The Hall of Fame' above the front door. As you open the door, imagine seeing a long corridor that is dark, but on both the left and right side, there are televisions on the wall leading up to the corridor lighting it up. Each TV is playing the inspirational highlights of you. It shows you achieving the main goals that you have previously written down.

Walk down a few steps to the first TV and watch yourself achieving the goal that you have set yourself. Perhaps this is to sign a promotional contract with your desired promotional company, or sell out a headlining show. See it being done on the TV. Then walk to the others and do the same.

This exercise can also be adjusted to help one of your current, most relevant goals. Imagine one of your current goals is to recover from a tough injury. For example, imagine you have injured your shoulder, and you are projected to be out for a few months.

See yourself walking into the hall and seeing one TV. Walk to the TV at the end of the hallway and see it playing footage of you doing well in physiotherapy and see the improvements before your eyes. Then let it show you walking into the ring and punching with that same shoulder and mightily knocking an opponent out.

This type of mental power is what allowed Conor to overcome an injury, which doctors said would keep him out for almost a year, in just a few short months.

HAVE A CHAMPION'S VISION

Act as the Champ Would Now

'I already feel like I'm living it, and then I just carry on day by day, already living the final goal, the goal of being [a] world champion. I already carry myself like a world champion. I already speak like I'm a world champion.'

Conor McGregor (before capturing a UFC world title)

Being a champion usually means when a fighter wins the championship belt. However, it is also important to remember that a fighter must actively live like a champion in everyday life. Being a champion is an active state of mind, not a fixed position.

There is no excuse not to act as a champion right now. After defining who you want to become, it is now time to live it out as much as you can. What would a champion be doing in his day-to-day activities, and what would his attitude be when doing it?

Perhaps it won't be just the way you want it to be immediately, but you can start to move towards it from this moment. This doesn't mean spending money, trying to look as flashy as the famous champions; it is more about the vibe of a true champion.

For example, the champions know how to manage their nerves. You may realise that you want to be able to manage your performance anxiety better. What are the steps required to make this possible? In what situations will you have to put yourself to achieve this? Get to it immediately.

Champ Affirmations:

The following affirmations are centred around achieving your desired goals in the future.

'I am going to win the WBC (World Boxing Council) championship belt (or substitute your preferred achievement). I will superbly reign over the division for years.'

'I am a Pay-Per-View superstar. I will make millions in the sport and entertain millions of fans around the world.'

The World Is Your Gym

As a busy fighter, Conor McGregor would always be on the move, flying from city to city and driving from town to town. However, he didn't let this stop him from training all the time. Conor McGregor adapted his training to the environment.

At beaches, airports, and car parks, he would fit his workout routine in. Most fighters don't do this, and this is where champions, like Conor, make the difference. You must always have your fighting cap on and view the world through the lens of the sport. This way, you will spot every opportunity that comes your way.

They say that seeing is believing, and it is true. But even when there is nothing to see, if you believe there is, you may end up seeing it. When you focus on negativity, even if there is none there, you will believe there is. Conversely, when you believe that possibilities lie all around you, you start to see how everything could be used to benefit you. A champion must see value where others see none.

For example, you injured your right hand in training, and you cannot use it anymore. Some fighters would see this as a cue to stay home and relax. However, what could be the value here? It could be that this is the perfect opportunity to master left-handed punches, as you cannot use your right. Train on the heavy bag by punching with your left hand for multiple rounds to improve your left jab or hook instead. Continuously, work on it. Where others didn't see an opportunity, you did.

Let's take a second example. Perhaps your coach is running an hour late to come and open the gym—meaning that you are stuck waiting outside until he arrives. Many fighters would see this as a cue to sit down and wait until the coach comes to open the door. They may take out their phones and check the latest nonsense on social media. They do not spot the opportunity to outdo others.

However, a champion-in-training will spot the value here or even create the value. Instead of waiting around and wasting time, you can take control of the situation. You could start the workout outside, as you wait. Warm up and shadow-box or take your rope out and start skipping immediately. Then when your coach comes, you are already warm, and no time has been wasted. You have used your time effectively, rather than letting it slip away, like most fighters do.

A CHAMPION'S HEART

Cus D'Amato & Young Mike Tyson: Effective Emotions

In 1980, a young kid named Michael Gerard Tyson had been brought to the legendary boxing coach Cus D'Amato by a man named Bobby Stewart. Bobby Stewart was the boxing coach who worked with young boys in the juvenile delinquent centre but had picked out Mike Tyson as the kid with the most potential.

Arriving at Cus D'Amato's gym, Mike was set to spar with Bobby for three rounds, and the youngster was determined to impress D'Amato. After seeing Tyson spar for the first time, Cus immediately prophesised, 'that is the next Heavyweight champion of the world.' Soon after, Cus took him in his fourteen-room Victorian mansion and dedicated himself to tutoring the youngster day in and day out.

Mike, who later became the most feared man in boxing, was originally a timid kid and was shy by nature. This was somewhat natural after the years of bullying and abuse he received, growing up in the rough area of Brownsville, Brooklyn. So the first mission for Cus was to peel away the residue of trauma, as Mike was left very insecure and with little belief in himself.

As Mike later put it, 'Cus wanted to reach me at the root. He was making me feel that I was worth something.' 'Go shadow-box and say, "Look how beautiful I look!"' he would tell Mike as he started breaking down those insecurities.

Cus was one of the few coaches that placed great emphasis on the mind of his fighters. He believed that a fighter cannot perform like a champion, if he doesn't feel good about himself. His daily compliments to Mike helped to make Mike feel good within his own body.

If you feel enthusiastic about yourself every day, it is easier to believe in yourself. Perhaps no one else in boxing history understood this more than Cus. Before even teaching a fighter, Cus always sat his fighters down for 'The Talk'.

'When I have a new boy, the first thing I do is give him a lecture,' he said. And no fighter was ready to be taught any boxing moves, until he had understood how to deal with his emotions. After receiving the lecture from Cus, the fighter would then be ready for Cus to get the best out of him.

Feel Like a Champion

As we have explored, what you think and what you say to yourself is extremely important. You must tell yourself you are great. But there must come a time where you truly feel it too, and your emotions begin to echo the affirmations that you say. It must become natural to feel like a champion, and you must develop a greater control of your emotions.

Emotions have a massive impact on a fighter's psyche. How you feel inside will influence what you can push yourself to do. How so? Uncontrolled emotions will dissuade you from being able to endure certain experiences. If your emotions control you, you won't be able to deal with an experience in which you feel bad, and you will instead choose the easy route that has the least discomfort.

For example, in June 1982, Mike Tyson was set to defend his Junior Olympic Heavyweight title against a fighter named Kelton Brown. Before the final, the pressure of the competition got to Mike. He was still dealing with his insecurities, and he doubted his ability to perform great in front of the audience. He broke down and cried outside the venue, and trainer Teddy Atlas had to comfort him.

Soon after, he reflected on what Cus had taught him about emotions. He transformed his insecurities into motivation and got himself together. By controlling his emotions, he could take the challenging route, instead of running from it. When Mike stepped foot in that ring, it took him one round to finish his opponent.

It is the most challenging route that has the most rewards. Specifically, fear, anxiety, and frustration are the most dissuasive feelings. They make it harder to learn from vital challenges, as the fighter will simply not participate. And without participating, you will stop yourself from sparring better fighters, training away from home, or having your technique constructively criticised. These experiences help your progress the most, so it is critical that you master your emotions.

Fighters that do participate in these challenges still won't know how to get the best out of every situation, if they do not have emotional control. You will mentally disengage yourself from the activity. Only the fighter who has belief will be fully engaged. He can commit his full attention to a tough task, and because of this, he is able to focus better.

On the other hand, if you are not mentally engaged, you will still feel the discomfort without getting any benefit from the participation. To lack emotional control is literally a waste of your time. You will feel uncomfortable *and* you won't be engaged, meaning you didn't learn what you could've got out of the situation. You will have gone through the discomfort for no reason.

Let's say two fighters fight in front of a large audience, and they are both anxious. The fighter who can manage his emotions can focus on what he must do, even with anxiety there. Despite feeling uncomfortable, he can fight to the best of his ability.

After adjusting to his opponent and fighting with success, he may find his anxieties start to slowly fade away, and his confidence escalates. His general belief mixed with discipline allows him to endure the short-term discomfort so that he can find a way to gain momentum.

Conversely, the other fighter cannot control his emotions. The discomfort can threaten his focus. He may focus on trying to avoid humiliation, rather than doing what it takes to adjust to his opponent.

Counterintuitively, this backfires as he lets fear take over. With no focus, he ends up taking even more punches because of it. Many fighters in this situation lose their cool even more, despite the fact that this is exactly what got them there in the first place. Losing their head, fighters often resort to lunging at their opponent angrily, which makes them easier to counter.

Unless he can get his emotions back under control and 'settle down', he will get into a negative cycle of taking punches, losing emotional control, and then taking more punches again. Situations like this are how you shoot yourself in the foot, all because you allowed your emotions to control you, rather than the other way around.

EMOTIONS OF A CHAMPION

As you become more experienced, you learn that it is a skill to be able to perform in the ring without too much emotional influence. Contrary to popular belief, will (or intense desire) does not beat superior skill. Emotions do not beat technique and strategy.

Will beats skill only if the fighter with skill lacks will to a huge extent and suffers from extreme lack of focus. Even then, however, the fighter with more will and less skill, needs to be at least around the same skill level as his opponent to pull off a victory. Keep working, and you will get to a point where your skill usually is good enough for the win. It is in times of deep struggle, when you need to call on your emotional will.

The real importance of will doesn't come as soon as the bell rings. Will is most important when you are faced with challenges that require an extra push. This especially is true in the gym, when you are faced with physical challenges, and failing (for the purpose of learning) is okay.

In the ring, will is *only* required when you are faced with a fighter who is on a similar level to you, and the bout becomes a contest of who wants it more. You should only let emotions take precedence over strategy, when you are trying to overpower a challenge, and it is important to know what positive emotions you should use to break down obstacles. The following are four emotions you should draw on to get you through tough times.

Pride in Your Past

In Mike's early days, Cus was pushing him hard in training. Unlike most amateurs, Cus had Mike sparring experienced professionals. Even though he was really young, Mike often gave the pros a good run for their money. Mike's favourite sparring partner was a talented fighter named Marvin Stinson, who was the chief sparring partner of Larry Holmes (the Heavyweight champ at the time).

Cus tried to get the Holmes camp to accept Mike as a sparring partner, to which Holmes stated, 'I won't train with amateurs.' This offended Cus, who knew that Mike could hold his own with the current champion. By offending Cus's pride, it only fuelled Cus into pushing Mike even harder so they would be ready to defeat him one day. Half a decade later, Mike would knock Holmes out in four rounds.

A champion should reject the idea of settling for less than his best. Pride refers to your sense of self-importance and how satisfied you feel with your past accomplishments. As we have covered, belief unlocks many possibilities, and allowing your pride to flow strengthens your level of entitlement to getting great results. Cus believed Mike was entitled to top-class sparring, and he took pride in demanding the best for his fighters.

When you are experiencing an obstacle, and you start to feel doubt setting in, harshly reject it and tell yourself you have done better before, so you can do better now. You've trained hard, your belief is high, and your ambitions are huge. You are too good to relent. This helps you to find the energy to resist giving up under high pressure.

Champ Affirmations – Reject Losing:

Allow some confidence to take place in the face of a challenge.

Repeat to yourself when you are struggling.

'I refuse to lose.'

'I'm a winner. I will always find the way.'

'I'm more superior than the obstacle in front of me.'

'I am too good to allow myself to fall victim to this challenge.'

Hope of Victory

Because Mike was living with Cus D'Amato every day, Cus had the chance to constantly tell Mike about their assigned mission of winning the Heavyweight championship. Everyday Cus would tell Mike *how* he would win the title and *why* he must win the title, so much so that Mike had no doubt in his mind that it would eventually happen.

Mike bought into Cus's belief that he would win the title one day. 'Lightning has struck me twice; I have another Heavyweight champion of the world (Floyd Patterson being his first),' he would randomly chuckle. Years before it had happened, Cus spoke as if it had already been written into the stars.

Cus was so descriptive about Mike's future reign that he would detail how the world would treat him and the lifestyle he would be able to live. 'People of royalty will know your name,' '"No" will be a foreign word to you,' he would tell Mike every day.

On one occasion, when Mike was doubtful about not being able to attract a girlfriend, Cus gave Mike a wooden bat and said,

'When you become [a] champ, you'll have so many girls chasing you [that] you'll have to beat them off of you!'

Hope is an emotion that helps a fighter to believe in his future, whether that future be the end of a match or the end of a career. Hope is your expectation that you will get the positive outcome you want. You can reinforce hope by affirming to yourself that 'I know I will win in the end' and combine this with the image of you winning.

Hope is important for a champion because it helps him believe in his visualisation of him conquering a problem. With belief in the end goal, you can then calmly set a plan to make it happen and see it through. Hope without action is hopeless. So, you cannot expect hope to make the difference; however, it does encourage you to do the things that will.

Hope and pride are emotions heavily connected to positive future expectations.

Love Your Passion

Cus loved the sport. He was addicted to boxing, and it was the only thing he knew. He never went to the movies, didn't watch TV shows, and cared little for famous people and popular trends. The great champions, like Joe Louis, were the only people about whom he would get excited to talk. His enthusiasm rubbed off on young Mike, and the two would spend hours discussing the stories of past fighters.

Contrary to mainstream belief, 'a happy fighter is a dangerous fighter', as Mike Tyson states. Fighters aren't all angry savages. Most boxers simply love expressing themselves through the sport. Boxing is your passion. If you believe boxing is your calling, you should be happy to box.

Fighting is taxing on the mind and body, but that is a small price to pay for the opportunity to participate in this great sport. Enjoy the process and don't stress on the destination. If you're doing the right things, it'll come. Few people have the chance to participate in their dreams. Enjoyment is much better than fighting with anger, frustration, or hate, and your mind will flow easier.

Inspiration in Challenges

Every time a young boy came to Cus's gym, Cus claimed that he was able to decipher the potential of the fighter within the first day. Upon entering the building of his boxing gym, there was a long staircase that led to the main room. If a fighter needed someone to take him to the gym and make that intimidating walk up the main room, Cus believed the boy would need a lot of mental work.

On the other hand, if a fighter was inspired enough to make that walk by himself, despite his nerves, then Cus knew he had something to work with. Most fighters seek to run from challenges. However, a true champion invites them. It excites him because he knows a reward awaits in the end.

A champion needs resistance to push him to greatness. This should inspire you because you will see it as the universe sending you an opportunity to show off your greatness. The opportunity is a compliment, so enjoy it. When these moments come, dig deep within your heart and allow yourself to feel inspired.

Champ Affirmations:

Great statements to make after a training session or when you're feeling depressed in training camp.

'I was born to fight. This is my sport.'

'I was made for this; every cell in my body loves fighting.'

'I am the happiest fighter in the world.'

Notice that love and inspiration are emotions heavily connected to a positive experience in the present moment.

THE BODY OF A CHAMPION

During the time that Cus served the military, he saw this as the perfect opportunity to harden his body, so it would be prepared for any challenge. Cus would push himself to sleep on the floor, shave with only cold water, stand for hours at attention, and set his alarm clock at random times each night so his body would get used to waking up on command.

Cus understood that his body should mirror the strength of his mind. Not only does a champion have a distinctive physique, or an impressive mind; he also has an amazing physiological state that is different to most people.

Specifically, the biology of a fighter is literally influenced by his mentality. When a champion thinks positively and believes in his self-worth, the body responds accordingly. The body attempts to reflect the high standards that you have set in your mind.

Science shows that people with a high level of mental control naturally have a stronger ability to relax the body, slow down their heart rate, and limit inner stress. This makes it easier to continue training hard. Those that feel positive more often than others will have better sleep with less stress to cause insomnia. This enables a fighter to recover quicker which is essential for a fighter who exercises intensely.

Overtraining is an issue for ambitious fighters who train often. They do the right thing by training hard, but then they also allow that hard work to be put to waste by not looking after their body.

If the body isn't in good shape, you will lose access to the endurance that you've worked to build up.

Other studies have shown that visualising positive physical results, such as seeing the ideal muscular body that you want to have, increases the effectiveness of your gym workouts, as your body releases signals within the nervous system that help with muscle regeneration. This is especially the case when the visualisation is backed by strong intent which helps to kick-start your physiology.

All of this is easier to do when you are filled with emotions like hope. Emotions can act as a source of energy for your body to realise these effects. This is why you must strive to gain emotional control; not only is it good for the mind but it also has physical effects.

Improving in this area will help you to suffer less in training camp, minimising the amount of physical stress you have to endure in the long term. Many fighters won't take it this far. However, as a champion-in-training, you mustn't fall into that trap. This is a perfect opportunity to create a gap between you and your competitors.

Action Affirmation: Relaxation

This affirmation should be used when your body is in stress, such as when you are out of breath (after a tough round has ended, after fast sprints or intense activity etc.), and your heart rate is high, or when you are starting to panic. Say it in your mind as you try to deeply breathe slowly, in the nose and out of the mouth.

'I am okay. Relax ... I am doing good.'

STAY HUNGRY

Anthony Joshua: Stay Motivated

Amongst the twenty-first-century kings of boxing, perhaps the most popular fighter of them all is Anthony Joshua (22-0, 21KO). Anthony Joshua was the former British Olympic gold medallist who defeated Charles Martin in his sixteenth pro fight in 2016 to win the IBF (International Boxing Federation) title. Two years later, Joshua added the WBA (World Boxing Association) and WBO (World Boxing Organization) titles to his collection by his twenty-first fight.

Representing the colours of the UK and having created a global brand, Anthony Joshua grew into a massive icon. Despite the whirlwind of success in a short period of time, however, 'AJ' continued to live by his 'stay hungry' and 'stay humble' mantras— and by doing this, he stayed motivated.

The British champ had probably been told how amazing he had done, and how he had 'made it' no fewer than a few thousand times after winning his championships. It could've easily gone to his head and made him egotistic. But those claims only drew swift rejections from the champion, who constantly repeated, 'I have a long way to go.' To stay motivated, you must stay level headed.

After placing the terrific right-hand straights on the chin of Charles Martin to capture his first world title, he was asked if he felt any different, to which he replied, 'Just a bit hungrier ... getting there was one thing, but maintaining it is going to be harder.'

In the couple years that followed his title win, AJ consistently demonstrated his humble mentality of staying grounded. Unlike many other champions after winning a major fight, he remained in great physical shape, continued to study the sport, and stayed active. Perhaps the greatest piece of evidence of his grounded head was the fact he chose to keep living with his mother even after securing multi-million paydays, knowing that his only priority is boxing.

By keeping your lifestyle humble, you force yourself to 'feed hunger and starve your distractions', as Anthony Joshua says. You can light up your passion for the sport and focus on what really matters: the fighting and the fighting alone. A champion-in-training must be extremely motivated. There is no exception to this rule.

The Champion's Engine

Motivation is like a champion's engine. No matter how nice the body of the vehicle is, the engine is what makes it move. Motivation drives you to take action, and action is what prepares you for fights; action is what ignites both progress and victory; action is what gets the results that you want. It must be done for months and years, and motivation allows you to do this.

When the body tires from continuously working, the average person becomes less willing to train. The constant effort feels extremely draining. Motivation is the internal drive which you use to keep you going.

A motivated fighter will work hard and stay consistent in training. Without a doubt, it is imperative that a champion-in-training works on having long-term motivation. If not, he will be outworked by the fighter who does.

In 2017, when Anthony Joshua defended his belts against the past king Wladimir Klitschko, he was in danger of losing the bout, going into the late rounds. Klitschko had knocked him down in the sixth round, after AJ scored a knockdown in the fifth. Afterwards, Klitschko was doing a good job of boxing from the outside range to avoid being excessively hurt. Going into the championship rounds, the fight was still competitive.

Joshua had already shown signs of fatigue and looked too tired to perform at his best. However, he was the younger, more motivated fighter. Despite being massively tired, he pushed past the pain barrier to spur on an energetic rally that put Klitschko on the canvas.

After getting up, Klitschko was then stopped via a TKO (Technical Knockout) victory, as the motivated Joshua hurled punch after punch at the fatigued Ukrainian to avoid leaving it to the scorecards. When the skilful man got tired, the motivated man had his chance, and he took it with a killer instinct.

Enthusiasm Drives Motivation

One component of motivation is enthusiasm. When a fighter lacks enthusiasm in his work, he fails to concentrate when he trains. Not only does lacking enthusiasm harm your focus in training, but it also stifles your performance at match time. When you are enthusiastic, you are more likely to have optimism. This state alone makes you more inclined to take action, because enthusiasm diminishes the 'cons' of taking action. The cons could include frustration, emotional pain, and time spent training etc. The more love you have for the sport, the less significant this is to you.

The good thing about enthusiasm is that it helps you to see the benefit in working hard, no matter how taxing it is, whilst lowering the downsides. If you genuinely enjoy training, then it won't feel like too much effort. An enthusiastic fighter enjoys it. As AJ has stated, 'There is no hard part about being a professional boxer; it's a blessing.' From this viewpoint, the world is a much more pleasant place, and it will reflect in your performance.

Champ Affirmation:

A favourite of Cus D'Amato's, used to reflect on the progress you have made and encourage future progress. Repeat twenty times in the morning and night.

'Everyday, in every way, I am getting better.'

LONG-TERM ENTHUSIASM

Staying Motivated

Motivation helps to uphold belief. When a fighter is motivated, he pushes himself into challenging situations with an energy that helps him to get the outcome he wants. Then as his effort is rewarded with victories, and he becomes accustomed to winning, he improves his mentality. These victories do not have to be major. It doesn't have to be winning a match or a medal.

A win could count as you completing a small task. This could be simply getting out of bed in the early hours of the morning for a five-mile jog, knowing that many other fighters would be lazy and stay in bed. Once you have completed the run, although you feel tired, you also feel satisfied with the effort you put in.

In the case that you don't get the result you want, you will still feel proud that you tried. As AJ said, 'My celebration is to hustle harder,' as opposed to a victory party after a match. When you enjoy the small wins, it makes the journey itself a pleasant experience.

To frequently experience this boost, you must set mini goals on a short-term basis, like weekly or even daily, so that you work towards bigger goals and feel proud. Your mind gets consistent evidence that reaffirms your claims to greatness. As you gain mini victories, you begin to forge Champ-set, and you trust yourself to regularly get the result you want.

Set minor goals that are challenging but are realistically achievable with some effort. For example, a short-term goal could be to run five miles for five days, instead of running for five miles every day for a month. Five miles for five days may be a challenge, but it is definitely achievable with a little bit of discipline.

Doing this dramatically cuts down the pressure on yourself and the perceived effort of the challenge. This gives you a boost in confidence more often after you complete it, helping to motivate you to do more.

Champ Affirmation: The 'Positivity Sandwich'

This verbal technique can be used to maintain enthusiasm when you critique yourself. The 'Positivity Sandwich' method describes a three-step process you can use to positively point out areas of improvement.

When criticising yourself, start off by telling yourself the thing you've done well. Next, tell yourself what you could've done better. Do not say what you've done bad, but what could be improved. This reframes your perspective from negative to positive.

Next, cap off the criticism with one thing in which you are starting to notice improvements. For example, say, 1) 'I threw the jab correctly.' 2) 'I could throw the right hand better.' 3) 'My footwork is getting better.' This is much better than simply saying 'I threw a terrible right-hand'.

By doing this, you coat your criticism with potential and keep enthusiasm. It is hard to learn when you are not enthusiastic. This is unique because it points out areas for improvement, whilst upkeeping hope. This is different to other common forms of criticism which are based totally on negative criticism—the one that will usually discourage and decrease a fighter's confidence.

OUTLAST TURBULENCE

Motivation Fluctuates

Due to the turbulent nature of a training camp, it is natural that your motivation will be up and down. It will be at different levels depending on what is going on in your career. Naturally, when things are going well, you will feel more motivated; and when things aren't going so well, your motivation may lessen.

The problem is that many boxers let motivation levels dictate how much effort they put in. You cannot fall into this trap. A champion cannot let his performance change as much as his emotions. Regardless of what happens, a champion is expected to perform at a high level. A fighter with a champion's mindset must believe in himself so much that he knows he can perform at a high level, no matter what he is going through.

Win or lose, 'you don't want to make a big deal out of it,' Joshua states. He also believes that 'When you win, you want to keep it balanced, and when you lose, you have to keep it balanced. You can't let it get to your head when you win, and you can't let it get to your heart when you fail.'

You cannot feel yourself into acting. You must act first, and then the feeling will come. At times, when you do not feel like fighting because of a lack of motivation, the best thing is to simply **do it anyway,** knowing that you will get into the mood later. The truth is that no matter how you feel, you must do what needs to be done.

There will come times when you don't want to wake up at 6 a.m. to run, or leave your friends for a late-night workout session, but you must. There will be times that you've experienced a harsh break-up or family feud. At other times, you will come back from a long lay-off and need to get used to the routine of training. Know that you can continue, despite the slight feeling of depression. At first, the task of fighting will feel like effort. But you will get into the feeling later. A three-hour session at the gym always seems tiresome before you actually get there. However, once you get into it, you gradually start to enjoy it.

Champ Visualisation: Public Workout with Fans

A routine that instils a sense of encouragement whilst you train.

At home: take a few minutes to sit down and imagine that a ring sits in the middle of a large dark hall. The ring lights shine above the ring, illuminating the canvas. You are standing in the arena, in your training gear, warmed up and ready to train. To each side of the ring, there are hundreds and thousands of raving fans, who have come to see you. They hold up signs in your name telling you they love you, they wear shirts with your face on it, and they all have their smartphones out trying to capture you. You are their inspiration.

Your coach is on the other side of the ring, with pads on, waiting for the bell to sound. As it does, you walk across the ring and work the combinations with your coach. With each punch, the audience cheers you on even more. You love hearing their support. You love knowing that your hard work excites them. After a few combinations, you walk to the rim of the ring, looking down on your fans with a confident smile, looking into their excited eyes. You think to yourself 'I was made for this'.

At the gym: when you are training, imagine the same scene. When you work on the heavy bag, when you spar, when you skip, when you do circuits, imagine you are in that ring surrounded by your dedicated supporters cheering for you. Imagine the noise and see the smiles.

With each move, they get even more excited. Do not slack off. Your fans are watching you, looking to be inspired by a hard worker. Don't sit down between rounds; stand up and imagine that you are pacing along the rim of the ring, looking down at your admiring fans.

When you are jogging: imagine that every few hundred metres there are a bunch of your fans waiting to cheer you on every time you start to tire. When you run past a bush of leaves, imagine it is your fans reaching out to get a touch of you; so hold your hand out and slap them five. On the last stretch when you are tired and slowing, imagine your fans on the side are cheering you on, wanting you to finish with a fast sprint. Do not let them down. Fall in love with the encouragement.

FIGHT WITH FEAR

Cus D'Amato And Young Mike Tyson: Don't Let Fear Hold You Back

It is impossible to mention fear without acknowledging the first person in boxing history to place a huge focus on it. Boxing coach Cus D'Amato is famous for mentoring young kids like Mike Tyson and Floyd Patterson from intimidated children to glorious champions, and he revolutionised the widely held view on fear.

Fear is one of the most challenging emotions a fighter must deal with, so it is inevitable that many try to avoid having it. However, Cus believed that 'a fighter has to know fear', if he wants to be a great champion. Fear isn't your enemy, unless you do not know how to control it. Left untamed, fear will taint your self-belief; but for a champion, 'fear is your best friend'. Managed correctly, it will be what adds the fuel to your fire.

Soon after Mike arrived at his home, Cus gave him a book called *In This Corner* by Peter Heller. It was a history book detailing the stories of past champions like Henry Armstrong and Jack Dempsey. The book was one of Mike's favourites because it helped him to learn how to deal with fear.

Mike would read stories about the fears that the great champions had experienced and how they had dealt with it. This inspired

Mike to accept that fear was normal, if someone as great as Jack Dempsey or Henry Armstrong could admit to being frightful.

Fear Is a Negative Illusion

When Cus was about fourteen, the Bronx newspapers were reporting a scary man called the 'Gorilla Man', who was hiding in alleyways and attacking the locals. Inevitably, many people were afraid of bumping into him at night and tried to avoid him. One night, he was taking a shortcut down a dark path and saw a figure that resembled the Gorilla Man.

Frightened, Cus wanted to run away in the opposite direction, but then he thought, 'If I run now, I'll never be able to take this shortcut again.' He challenged his fear and went ahead. He was relieved to find that the Gorilla Man was just a tree with most of its branches cut off, with a silhouette that resembled a gorilla. It was a scary illusion. From then on, when confronting fears in the future, he would tell himself, 'That's just a tree in my path.'

Fear is an emotion that forces you to make bad predictions about what could happen in the future. It makes you apprehensive and unsure about what is to come. Fear will cause you to doubt your chances in the ring, as you question yourself and focus on the negative.

'Do I have enough to win?' 'What if I lose?' 'I don't want to be embarrassed,' 'I don't want to get hurt,' 'I don't think I'll be good enough'. These are the words that ring in the mind of fighters, as they second-guess themselves.

There is no fighter that ever lived without experiencing fear, and the fighter who tells you that he is the exception is most likely lying. Most coaches would also agree, you never lose fear. As Cus D'Amato stated, a fighter will be as fearful in his hundredth fight, as he was in his first ever fight.

The only difference between the newbie and the experienced fighter is that the latter learns how to deal with it so that it doesn't hinder his performance. A champion finds a way to let his fear work for him, making his performance even better than what it could be.

The problem with fear is that it is an illusion. When we feel fear, it is a reaction to something that we think could happen in the future. Yet it isn't about something that it is happening now, in the present moment. It doesn't have any real effect on you in that particular moment.

For example, imagine a fighter is waiting in the dressing room an hour before his fight. In the weeks running up to this bout, he has trained extremely hard for an opponent who is a step up in class. As the bout gets closer, the reputation and physical appearance of his opponent may seem intimidating, so the fighter starts to allow fear to slowly seep in. Uncontrolled, his fear will cause him to magnify the bad things that 'could' happen.

However, no matter how fearful he may be at this point, if we shift the focus on what bad is happening to him *now*, he will see that he doesn't have as much to worry about. Is his opponent punching him now? Is he in any pain *right now?* The wait before a fight is the most anxious part, yet it is technically the safest part of the fight.

Don't be a fake expert. Step into the ring and let the experience tell you if you can win. When you take a deep breath and focus on what is happening in the current moment, you will see that there is little to fear most of the time.

Fear is a negative illusion of the future. Feeling fear is only practical when you are trying to overcome a *current* challenge. It is a waste of energy when you allow fear to increase your worries *before* anything has actually happened.

Fearing doesn't make a difference to what you must do. You will still have to step inside of the ring, and fear won't make the opponent an easier target. In fact, if your rival gets a whiff of your fear, he will gain a confidence boost, and then it will make him even harder to face.

Champ Affirmations: Self-Encourage

Talk yourself up when you are feeling fearful. Particularly powerful when used on the day of a match, and when you are about to make your ring walk.

'I can do this.'

'I've prepared for this moment, and I am going to perform brilliantly.'

'I was made for this; nothing on this planet can stop me.'

The Right Perspective: Reframing Fear

Fear was one of the main focuses of 'The Talk' given to new fighters. Cus wanted his fighters to know that fear can have a paralysing effect only if it is left uncontrolled. Fear can work for you, being your 'best friend' when it is controlled. As Cus taught his fighters, 'Fear, like fire, must be controlled and, once it gets out of control, like fire, could destroy everyone around.'

You cannot get rid of fear, but the good news is you can manage it. By shifting your perspective on how it can help you, it can be of use to you. There is a difference between using fear to warn you of an emerging threat so you can respond to it accordingly and allowing fear to make you shy away from the challenge.

A mental technique you can use to help you take control of fear is **reframing.** Reframing means to switch your perspective of a situation. Encourage yourself to look at the glass as half full, rather than half empty. For every one challenge, there are multiple perspectives. Instead of giving a situation a negative interpretation, make the effort to see the positive. This will limit unnecessary fear.

Change the words you use to describe the challenges you face so you can change how you will feel about it. This doesn't mean lie to yourself. In fact, lying is uncontrolled fear that makes you delusional. Be realistic about the challenge, but simply look to what you can do, rather than what you can't. It doesn't help at all to focus on the negative.

Champ Affirmation: Reframing Examples

When you are waiting in the dressing room before a match, turn your pessimistic statements into confident ones.

Instead of saying, 'My opponent looks like he is in great shape; he probably hits hard,' say, 'My opponent looks like he is in great shape. He may be a hard hitter, but I've trained hard enough to endure anything he could give.'

Instead of saying, 'I hope I will do good,' say, 'I have prepared superbly. I know I will perform at my best.'

Substitute 'there are so many people watching in the audience; what if I mess up?' with 'there are so many people watching in the audience; I'm excited to entertain them with my skills!'

Instead of saying, 'What if I didn't do enough to get in shape?' say, 'I did my best with the time I had; I'm ready!'

Instead of saying, 'I feel nervous. I don't want to fight!' say, 'I feel nervous. This is a sign that I'm excited to fight.'

USE PAST LESSONS TO FUEL THE FUTURE

Past Pain

Young champions step into the ring as a means of running away from the harsh reality of their life. Looking at the Hall of Fame, you'll find that most of the sport's greatest went through painful experiences as they grew up. Rather than letting these experiences shape the rest of their life for the bad, it was their driving force.

Growing up in an environment where you suffer from things like relative poverty, bullying, loneliness, abuse, or other painful experiences, can lead to a fearful approach to life. This means that fighters live life to *not* lose, rather than trying to risk it all *to get the win*.

However, a champion-in-training will not let the fear of the unknown keep him down. Instead, he will allow the pain of the past to give rise to his motivation, and it will make him fearless.

If you are amongst those that hold onto past pain and let it dictate your lack of action, be aware that this will hold you back. You will have to make a leap of faith soon if you want success. Instead, tell yourself that the pain of the past is the perfect motivation to fight for a better life.

It is the perfect springboard to a better future. Not only will your achievements change your own life, they will also change the lives of the others who share that same pain. They will have a leader to look to and use as an inspirational example. So, if you cannot be fearless for yourself, force yourself to be fearless for them.

Look Back on How Far You've Come

As time goes by and life knocks you down repeatedly, it often makes you question yourself. However, a fighter who questions himself will have no killer instinct in the ring. He will train with less ambition, and he will perform with timidity. This is not the approach of the champion, and you will not be successful with this mindset.

Look at how far you have come, despite the losses that you may have endured. Use it as fuel. When we have spent time training and practising, we forget how far back we started. However, this can be a great source of confidence because you draw inspiration on the progress that you personally have made.

When you are taking on your latest challenge, you may have a quick loss of belief and boost of fear. At this point, remember that you have been in a similar position before and you found a way. So, you will do the same now and find a way.

Champ Visualisation: the 'Mirror Admiration' Exercise

A great routine to do during/after workout sessions, especially leading up to a fight and in the dressing room before a match. A favourite of Sugar Ray Leonard's.

As you warm up/down, pace slowly by the mirror, breathing slowly and getting into a focused state. Embody the persona of a champion with tunnel vision, and loosen up by lightly jogging on your feet. Start to shadow-box at the mirror and admire your muscular form.

Look at your arms, legs, and torso and be impressed by your body, which is fit for battle. Feel every motion of the punches, as you shadow-box; every step, as each foot hits the ground; and focus on your intent to win in spectacular form.

Next, stop shadow-boxing, but keep motion in your feet by stepping forward and back slightly in your boxing stance, or lighten the intensity of the shadow-boxing, and look into your own eyes. See those eyes as the eyes of a magnificent champion, who is focused on taking care of business. See yourself as an entirely different person—the champion who refuses to lose.

Train Your Focus

'Your mind is not your friend; I hope you know that, right?' Cus would tell Mike. Your mind is naturally inclined to look out for potential risks so you can avoid them. This means your mind is constantly being taught to think in a fearful tone, and this is opposite to the thinking of a champion.

Train yourself to spot the potential success in everything. Otherwise, it is likely that you will naturally train yourself to spot limitations instead. There is a part of the brain that is specifically responsible for where you put your selective focus. If you are coming from a negative mental zone and choose to think about what can go wrong, you are training your brain to look out for the limitations in your environment.

You are becoming a master in looking out for the things you should fear, magnifying your views on the risks around you. You need to be able to step into situations which are out of your comfort zone if you want to progress. By exaggerating your fears, you will discourage yourself from doing what is required to become a better fighter.

Conversely, the fighter who is operating from a positive mental zone, choosing to think about what could go right, automatically trains his brain to filter through positive interpretations of his environment.

You need to turn everything into an advantage in some way or another. This is impossible with a brain trained to pick out negativity. With positive focus, however, you will keep pushing past your comfort zone.

CHASE THE DREAM

Jack Johnson, the Black Heavyweight Hope

Perhaps the champion who has proven he had the most belief, in the sport's history, was Jack Johnson (73-13-10D-5NC, 40KO). Born in a time of furious racism in the United States of America, Jack Johnson's achievement of being the first black Heavyweight champion in 1908 could be described as the most monumental accomplishment in the sport. This is especially true considering the flashy, flamboyant personality he exuberated, in a time where African-Americans were murdered for as much as walking down the road confidently.

Without hope, it would have been impossible for Jack Johnson to claim the title, despite beating everyone in the division, many of them more than once. Jim Jeffries who was the current Heavyweight champion at the time promised that 'for as long as I could help it, a black fighter will never be the Heavyweight champion of the world'. He was supported by the white media as he rejected Johnson's calls to offer him a shot at the title.

On one occasion, Johnson boisterously followed Jeffries into a bar, and in front of tipsy onlookers, he loudly demanded that he get his title shot. Jim replied by slapping 25,000 dollars on the table and offered to fight Johnson in the downstairs cellar. Jim arrogantly stated to Johnson, 'If you can manage to walk back up the stairs, you can keep the money.' With pride, Johnson replied, 'I ain't no cellar fighter.'

Johnson continued to fight on in the hope of getting an official title. When Jeffries retired, Johnson still didn't receive a shot at the vacant title, and it was again contested between two white challengers instead. However, Johnson's patience finally paid off, when he managed to force the later champion into giving him a title shot.

The then-champion was Canadian Tommy Burns, who agreed to fight Johnson as long as he was paid $30,000 (compared to Johnson's much lower $5,000). Johnson didn't care; he was finally getting the title shot after ten long years of professional fighting.

In December 1908, he savagely stopped Tommy Burns and became the first black Heavyweight champion. It was so brutal that the police ordered the match recording to be stopped, right before they stopped the bout. The police did not want the sight of a black fighter beating a white fighter to reach mass America, but it didn't matter now.

Everyone knew how definitively Johnson had defeated Burns. Despite all of the resistance Johnson had encountered over the years, he was finally etched into boxing history. If Johnson would have given up, no one could have blamed him. Many fighters would, but Johnson kept fighting on with hope, and it paid off in the end.

The Opposite of Fear

As we have stated, hope is an important trait in the fight game. Without hope, any belief you have will be a temporary moment, rather than a long-term expectation. Hope and fear are similar emotions. They are both totally based on what *could* happen in the future, rather than what currently *is* happening. Fear and hope are two different sides to the same coin.

The difference is that fear is based on a worrying prediction. On the other hand, hope is based on positive expectation. When you are hopeful, you are more likely to believe in what you are trying to do. Your imagination will soar, and you will set high standards. Being hopeful encourages you to think outside the box when you are trying to force a result. This is crucial if you do not receive much positive encouragement from those around you.

Hope helps you to believe that you are better than the limited role the world has forced on you. When you have hope, it doesn't seem so crazy that you should train harder or put in more effort than anyone else, because you expect to reach your goals. Hope makes you crazy if you *don't* train according to what your goals require.

Hope is Better than Fear

Since hope makes a fighter dream of something that isn't technically true yet, you could say hope is irrational. We may dream about knocking out a great foe in front of a raving crowd, but it hasn't happened yet. Just like with the things we fear; it isn't happening yet.

Before it has happened, it is nothing but a thought, yet to make an appearance into reality. But unlike fear, which is just as irrational, hope helps you to make this thought happen. Fear discourages belief; hope encourages it.

The path to greatness is a long harsh one. Many young fighters stay in the sport with no hope and pay for it later when things get difficult. Mastery doesn't take weeks or months. It takes many years of hard work. Hope allows you to be patient.

When Jack Johnson was continually blacklisted from the Heavyweight title, he literally chased Burns around the globe taunting him into giving him a shot. From San Francisco to New York, or from London to Paris, Johnson followed Burns wherever he went, making Burns cave into the pressure. By chasing Burns around the world, he was chasing his dream.

There was no logical reason to expect that he would ever get the title, but his tremendous hope that it could happen one day, made him believe in the myth. Fuelled by this belief, he did what he needed to do to turn the myth into reality.

There were other black Heavyweights (like Joe Jeanette and Sam Langford) that also deserved a title shot, but Johnson was the only one that made it happen. Had he given up hope, he would never have put in so much effort to make it happen.

Champ Visualisation: Post Victory

At home: see that victory has already happened. Take two minutes to imagine being at the post-fight press conference after you have won the championship. After defeating your opponent in supreme fashion, the reporters want to hear from the champ.

Visualise opening the door to a hall where the conference is taking place. As you open the door and look in front, there is an elevated stage with a long table covered in black tablecloth and a stand with a mic for you to speak on.

As you walk up the steps to go to the mic, the reporters are applauding you with smiles on their faces, as they just saw you make history. Go up to the stand and look back at the reporters in the audience. Your friend is behind you, holding up your belt.

They ask you, 'How does it feel to be a champ?' You reply with confidence, 'It feels just right; the belt is where it belongs.' 'Could you have ever imagined that you'd one day be here with the belt?' they ask again. You knew it would happen all along. 'It would be criminal if I weren't. This is exactly what I worked for.' They ask you more questions, as cameras flash, and you answer. You then thank them for their time and walk away, down the steps and back through the door that you came.

BE PATIENT

Your Shot Will Come

Hope is also necessary in times of losses. Many fighters, including the sport's legends, do not win their first high-profile fight. Later, however, by performing even better, they are able to prove that those losses were flukes. The key to making a better comeback is to remain hopeful through those setbacks so that you can get to the next level.

Boxing history shows that the hopeful fighter is willing to do more to put himself in a position to get him his 'shot', compared to those with little hope. Greatness requires patience. Hope is the emotion that allows you to stick it out until your shot comes. Your mentality should believe that 'it is only a matter of time'.

It is also much easier to be patient when you believe the outcome is a foregone conclusion. You must believe on the deepest level that it will happen. Time is a filter that weeds out the pretenders.

Most fighters think they want to be the champion, but few fighters prove this with their willingness to be patient. If you want it bad enough, time should be a minor inconvenience for you. In fact, if you have both belief and patience, you will view the wait as a fantastic opportunity to prepare for a lengthy reign at the top. This is the time to get ready and make sure that when your time comes, you will take full advantage.

Champ Affirmations:

Talk with expectation that your goals will be complete. Great for when you are on long runs or when you are feeling the strain of a training activity on the heavy bag or other activities.

'I can do it.'

'I am going to lift that belt; it will be mine.'

'I can buy all the things I want when I'm reigning champion.'

'This effort is going to pay off.'

Be specific, and adjust the affirmation based on what you personally want.

For example: 'After I'm champ, I'll have no problem buying the four-bedroom house I want in Beverly Hills.'

Don't Give Up

Patience should never be accompanied by a lack of action. Patiently waiting for your time in the right way means training hard, whilst creating and taking opportunities. Do not mistake patience for the idea of operating at a mediocre level with a passive attitude.

Many fighters mistakenly think that if you just simply wait with desire alone, an opportunity will come to you. When it comes to opportunities, never wait and always create. A champion must be proactive.

You must seek to improve every single day. This is the right way to take action. Train as much as you can and study boxing often. Like Johnson, you must actively chase your dream each and every day.

Persistence is key because it increases the chances of you succeeding at something. For example, let's say that you are trying to practise a new footwork technique while sparring. However, the technique is complex and difficult, so you won't get it right the first time.

If you are hopeful that you can eventually do it properly as long as you keep persisting, it won't be hard to carry on until you get it right. It may be at the fifty-fourth time of trying, when it suddenly clicks and feels right. Then once you 'get it', you are able to do it correctly consistently, but without persistence, you wouldn't have made it until that fifty-fourth time.

Knowing you will get the outcome you want will extend your endurance when you start to tire. Your body may want to give up, but a hopeful mind will force the body to use every bit of energy to go on longer.

Without hope, a fighter is less likely to do this, because he won't want to go through the discomfort of trying. When you are hopeful, the short-term pain is worth it, because you know it will lead to the ending reward.

Fighters often feel discouraged when they persist through a challenge, because they will view the energy used as a waste if it doesn't pay off. This isn't an issue if you are hopeful; you will see any necessary pain as purposeful. A hopeful fighter will be able to outlast his peers, as he can access all of his energy supply.

Champ Visualisation: Hold the Belt

Everywhere: a mental routine to be done anywhere, whether it be at home, or in your workouts. It is especially good at the end of a training session.

Imagine that you have the title belt in your possession. Envision that you literally have it on your shoulders. At the end of a training session, walk slowly back and forth, and imagine that the belt is on your waist. Sense how the material would feel and how heavy it would be. At the end of a sparring session, feel the belt over your right shoulder, and know that it belongs to you. When you are being interviewed, imagine the belt being on your lap, and talk with extreme confidence.

PART 2: CREATE YOUR REALITY

YOUR WORLD MAINTAINS YOUR BELIEF

'It's Not about How Hard You Hit'

'Let me tell you something you already know. The world ain't all sunshine and rainbows. It's a very mean and nasty place, and I don't care how tough you are; it will beat you to your knees and keep you there permanently if you let it! You, me, or nobody, is gonna hit as hard as life. But it ain't about how hard you hit; it's about how hard you can get hit and keep moving forward; how much you can take and keep moving forward. That's how winning is done! Now if you know what you're worth, then go out and get what you're worth, but you gotta be willing to take the hits!'

Rocky Balboa, from *Rocky VI* (2006)

One of the most inspirational speeches you are ever likely to hear. Despite being a fictional character, there was no fiction to that statement. The first part of *Automatic Ambition* is based on what you need to say to and about yourself to grow the champion's mindset. Yet, that is half the work. The next step is to let Champ-set shape the reality you have envisioned.

Champ-set is the framework that enables you to push forward. You cannot rely on others to take on any initiative to do this. This is the responsibility of you and you only. Your inner belief by itself means nothing if you don't use it to literally craft the world around you. Champ-set unlocks the ability to do this.

To come from nothing to something, means that you must literally take a thought which only exists in yourself and have it influence the world around you. To do this, you must start to gather the experiences that build you into the person you want to be.

These experiences may include skilfully beating lesser opponents, gaining supporters, or being supported by prominent managers and promoters. All of these things add up to help you become the champion you want to be. It is impossible to achieve your dreams if you do not have the actual ability to change your environment.

You are not trying to fight against the world; ultimately, you are fighting against the things that stops the world from working for you. Thinking and feeling like a champion gives you the qualities of one, but using those qualities to get the championship is another story. The practical methods needed to achieve this are all covered in the last part of the book.

In the following chapters, we will touch on practical aspects that a champion must manage effectively.

You must improve on the following: dealing with **distractions** and blocking negativity**,** gathering **support,** persisting through **struggle**; your **attitude** and how to take opportunities, and **accepting** your natural circumstances to make it work for you. These are the tools you need if you wish to build your own reality.

We will look at practical methods based on what the boxing champions have done. History shows that the greatest fighters achieved their own results with specific tools. The same tools can work for you and influence the progress of your career. From Muhammad Ali to Floyd Mayweather and from Jack Dempsey to Mike Tyson, every one of these champions had to adjust their daily living to achieve the things that they did.

The transmuted belief of those champions resulted in them being able to: learn at a faster rate, learn more skills than other fighters, and train more intensely with more motivation and a general increase in confidence.

The best practice for the ring is life. For a champion-in-training, this means he cannot just step inside the ring and expect to perform magnificently. His inner vision in the ring is to defeat his opponent. However, translating this inner vision into the outer world of reality is a skill that you forge whilst you train and progress physically and mentally. Then, once you step inside the squared circle (boxing ring), you can let out the effects of Champ-Set.

Champ Assignment – Tell the World and Add Accountability

An essential part of successfully constructing your dreams is to voice it. Communication via speaking is like the bridge between thinking it and doing it. When you are thinking about your dream, the vision is solely inside your mind. Once you have done it, the goal has been made into reality. But it can also be made to be put into the world before you have time to fully complete it by simply voicing it. The act of saying it aloud still puts it out there. It is less tangible than the finished project but more tangible than just the thought itself.

Projecting your goals is important because it starts to encourage you to make it real. Loudly speaking about your dreams ignites the start of the project, so you will naturally want to get to work and finish the job. This is especially the case once you say it to people around you, and you create an expectation for yourself to get it done.

Once people know precisely what it is that you want, they will attach you to the outcome that you have predicted. Doing this gives you a sense of accountability. Now you have to get it done because that was the expectation that you put in their minds. In the first section, we spoke about creating this expectation for yourself. But now, we must put it out into the world.

From now on, start speaking confidently and vividly about what it is that you will achieve in boxing. Let everyone around you know what it is that you want, and do not be ashamed about it at all. On social media, and with friends, let the world know what is about to take place. Many people will think of you as arrogant, and many will say you are crazy. But these are the people that cannot be considered friends.

Many people will have different responses to what you are saying. But you have to know your perspective and stick with that no matter what happens. If you continuously switch up what you feel according to other people, you will be like a lone leaf in the wind. So do not let their opinion have a substantial effect on you. On the other hand, the people that support your vision are your real friends. The point is to put yourself in a position where you have pressure to perform and live up to an expectation. That way, you will be more likely to stay focused in training camp and do everything you can to make your claim come true.

Champ Affirmation: Say It & Do It

When talking to others, you will be tempted to dull your belief around people who find your ambition offensive, for no other reason than the fact that it highlights their limitations. Start to make both yourself and the people around you feel comfortable hearing you voice your ambition.

When someone asks you what you want to be when you are older or what goals you have in five years, do not say, 'I guess I'll try to see what I can do with boxing'; rather say, 'I expect to be fighting in the Olympics,' (if that is your goal).

When someone asks, 'Do you think you can become a world champion?', you should reply, 'Of course I can; there's no doubt that one day I'll be fighting for the title.'

Do not defend your goals; merely express them. If the vision you have is real to you, then you shouldn't let others make you feel weird about it. Otherwise, this tells your mind that the goal isn't as real as you are claiming it to be. Believe that anyone else who doubts you is the weird one. They are crazy for not seeing what you see. Give it time; you will soon show them.

'There is no separating who we are in sports to who we are in the outer world.'

George Mumford

DISTRACTIONS & DOWNFALLS

Mike Tyson & the Circus

During the last half-decade that capped off the 1980s, Mike Tyson (50-6-2NC, 44KO) had obliterated every pretender to the Heavyweight championship throne with the force of a titan. The tyrannical world champion, who remains the youngest Heavyweight champion to this day, earned his place in Heavyweight history after around six years of hard work resulted in a two-round demolition of Trevor Berbick in November of 1986 for the WBC title. Unfortunately, his mentor Cus D'Amato passed away a short time before Tyson claimed the Heavyweight crown, so Cus didn't get to see his reign over the division.

Fast forward to February of 1990 in the Tokyo Dome when Tyson took on 42-1 underdog James 'Buster' Douglas. Somehow the massive underdog had landed a series of punches that reduced Tyson to a fallen champion, who could not get up to beat the 10-count in the eighth round. How could it be? What had changed? Why was this once-dominant king now an ex-champion?

The answer is simple. It came down to a change in his lifestyle that sowed the seed of his future demise. It took a couple of years for it to affect his abilities, but his distractive lifestyle eventually caught up with him. Rewind to two years before that Douglas defeat, in 1988, and Tyson's life had begun to fall apart outside of the ring.

In the summer of 1988, the Heavyweight champ had got into a street fight with his former opponent Mitch Green at half past four in the morning in Harlem, New York. He fractured his right hand on the face of Mitch, leading to the postponement of his proposed showdown with Englishman Frank Bruno at Wembley Stadium. Only a month later, Tyson crashed his BMW into a tree in Catskill, allegedly angered and stressed from a domestic dispute with his wife Robin Givens.

A few months later in December of 1988, Tyson fired his long-term trainer Kevin Rooney, who himself was schooled in the Cus D'Amato arts. Eleven days before his fight with Frank Bruno in February of 1989, Tyson flew to the Dominican Republic to finalise his hectic divorce to Robin Givens.

Distraction after distraction happened. It took two more fights until the drama caught up with him. Tyson himself later said that the personal problems don't affect a fighter straight away, so he couldn't see it coming, 'but it's the aftermath of the personal problems that get you'.

If a fighter is serious, it should be shown in his dedication in training and the clear-mindedness of his routine. Being dedicated means you must remove the negative energy that threatens to hold you back from being fully immersed in the profession of fighting.

Remove the Distractions

If you want to perform like a champion, then your thoughts and feelings should reflect a champion's. Your daily affirmations determine these thoughts and feelings. However, the biggest natural affirmation is your environment and daily activities. These are your 'environmental affirmations', and they automate the default content of your thoughts and feelings.

What you do every day, or your environmental affirmation, will influence your thoughts more than anything else. So being constantly distracted will supersede your affirmation and visualisation routines.

You must stay focused every day to automate the cycle of positive thinking. If you engage in distractive activities, it will taint your training routine, eating habits, and career decisions. Your environmental affirmations will be negative.

Distractions are like shackles to an ambitious fighter, and the problem is that despite consciously knowing that you shouldn't be distracted, it can be incredibly hard to fight it. When a fighter's habitual thinking has been triggered by a distractive lifestyle, he trains his mind to value things that do not help his ambition.

When Mike was 'preparing' for his match to 'Buster' Douglas, he was partying, skipping training, waking up late for runs, eating bad foods, and so on. A distracted mind will justify why it allows you to do things you know that you shouldn't. So, it is important to understand how to limit this.

Prevention Beats Cure

The first key to defeating distractions is to become aware; know when you are losing focus. This should naturally bring enough attention to it to create inner guilt. It will automatically bring attention to what you should be doing, and you will snap out of it if you are in a motivated state.

Before his Douglas match, Mike allowed many sources of distractions to take root, which limited any motivation he could've had. From his new promoter Don King and the new trainers that couldn't push him to the friends who had surrounded him, the circumstances made it easy for him to train in the wrong way.

The right way to stay focused is to remove or manage the potential sources of distraction in your life—if they are under your control, how could they have any damaging effect? First, however, you must know what these distractions are.

SOURCES OF DISTRACTIONS

SOCIAL MEDIA

In an online world with technology taking over, a major distraction is social media. This includes the apps that we use on a daily basis to fight boredom (such as Facebook, Instagram etc.). The problem is that hundreds of hours can be wasted when you are scrolling through purposeless media that doesn't help your boxing goals.

At first, it may seem hard for those with an addiction, but you must control it. This is especially the case if you are looking at content that isn't boxing-related or motivating. A fighter has to moderate his intake of tabloids and social media.

Most media content usually represents the thoughts of the 'average' distracted person, rather than that of the ambitious person. Most of the time, it is full of discouragement and hate.

Repeatedly taking in the beliefs of unambitious people will encourage your mind to live out those same thoughts. If you are watching goofy videos all day long, it becomes more difficult to keep a killer instinct. A fighter should have the thoughts of a champion replaying in his head. Media content wrongly used can prevent this.

Champ Assignments for Social Media

The 'Triple 3' Rule (33.3%): media that is boxing-related, or helpful to your progress, is good for you. So rather than limiting your intake, regulate the media that you are consuming. The 'triple 3' (33.3%) rule is a way you can do this.

Split the time you spend on media, social media, and the like, into three categories. Make sure that 33.3% of your content consumption is educational (e.g. boxing or business/ marketing books, studying boxing or workout videos), so you are continually learning. The next third of your time on media is inspirational (e.g. Rocky/Creed movies, entertaining fights, interviews of success stories), so it helps you stay motivated. Lastly, make the last 33.3% of your time based on entertainment. This could be anything, including the stuff you find fun, so that you avoid mentally burning out.

Build Your Empire—Create: alternatively, instead of consuming content, why not create content? Be a creative influencer. Establish the story that you want people to know about you, and tell that story through social media so that you begin to build up your own profile. Make content that is either entertaining, educating, or inspiring every day, and your follower base will grow.

Build Your Empire—Connect: social media was made for the purpose of connecting people. Network with potential fans, fighters, and other promoters to build up your reputation, power, and popularity. DO NOT rely on other people to do it. Do it yourself. The control is in your hands, and you are not at the mercy of promoters like you would have been decades ago. Converse and engage with many people daily so you can literally build up your own name.

Haters: one thing Cus taught Mike was to practice getting used to people giving him criticism, and remaining unaffected by it. Figure out the best way you personally deal with criticism. Some fighters do best by blocking it out altogether (e.g. block people online or do not read posts or comments).

Other fighters feel better addressing it, but it is important that you never take it seriously. Fight back with humour, which makes you look more confident anyway.

NAYSAYERS

Close Associates with No Ambition

Watch the people with whom you closely surround yourself. This includes the friends, family, and other authority figures who have great influence over the decisions we make. Specifically, if these people have a mindset that is in conflict with your goals, then it is a problem.

Many people (including fake experts) naturally like to dominate their surroundings with their own beliefs. Now if you allow this type of people into your world, and they have limiting beliefs, they will infect you with those same beliefs too.

Many of the people around us do not wish to see us change. It is a natural human trait. Becoming a champion, however, requires a lot of change. Many people will never understand the need to take such a brutal sport so seriously. They are often attracted to what is safe and comfortable. But the safe fighter doesn't win championships; the fighter who can take risks does. When a fighter is around people who lack ambition, he risks his standard of performance dropping if they have a heavy influence over him.

One of Mike's problems was that his close associates couldn't communicate the urgency of hard work after Cus D'Amato died. As Butch Lewis (the promoter of Tyson's opponent Michael Spinks) said, 'There was no guy there to say "[Get] back on track Mike. Stop; that's the wrong thing to do. You should be doing this; you shouldn't be doing that."' If no one around you understands the requirements of success, then no one is there to guide you to stay on the right path.

Distraction can also come from other fighters. Although many fighters dream of massive achievements, few fighters actually believe in them coming true, which will show through their own lack of discipline in training. If you allow yourself to match the energy of those fighters around you, your performance levels will drop too.

Champ Assignment: Watch out for people that do not push you to do better. Do not complain about your hardships to people who would advise you to give up after hearing them. That is not the advice you need to hear. They may not have bad intentions, but because of their lack of ambition, they will not know how to motivate you into effective action.

Distance yourself from people who discourage you. If you cannot or do not want to, ensure the topic of conversation or the activities you do are totally unrelated to boxing. This holds true even if it is your family, friends, or your romantic relationship.

Work or Academic Environments

Being a fighter doesn't exactly fit with the mainstream expectations of the world. Our parents and elders would much prefer that we grow up to be 'lawyers, doctors, or bankers' so that we can ensure a safe life.

To most, the life of a fighter seems like a tough life of struggling to 'make it', and even knowing that some fighters do 'make it', they will still complain about the health risks you'll endure. Although this is a real issue, thinking about it will not make you a successful fighter; a positive mindset with belief of success will.

A fighter must be totally different to most people. In environments such as the normal 9-5 workplace or in school, 'average' traits are normal, and ambition can even sometimes be offensive to some people. You may be a fighter who is still in the process of 'making it'. So, you might still be in this environment as you work your way up. Be wary of how this can damage your championship spirit.

Plan B

Fighters are constantly told that they should have a Plan B, which means to have a 'back up job' in case you fail to become a successful boxer. This advice usually comes from people who believe that a safe job is the best option.

However, the problem is that in these environments of professionalism, such as workplaces and schools, the people there do not share your vision. Much of the advice that you receive will differ from advice that you'd get from people in the sport.

Let's look at an example: Many times, a fighter may have to save his money to invest in his career. This could be for ticket marketing, making fan merchandise, and other match expenses. The more he can invest, the more often he will be able to fight, and the more he can grow his career.

This is the reality for a fighter who hasn't yet got serious support from a promoter. However, the people with a safe job rarely have to deal with the reality of investing in themselves, let alone be even aware of it.

They will give you advice based on what *they* would do, not necessarily what *you* should do when making career decisions. They won't understand why you don't spend your money on a nice car or the latest trends, and why you spent it all on training expenses.

People in these environments will naturally see the best path as being 'a respectable professional' in the corporate world. This is why they picked that route for themselves. Naturally, they will try to convince you that this is the smartest choice. 'It is good to have a Plan B,' they will say. The problem is that by having a Plan B, you divide your energy, rather than putting it all into your craft.

In addition to this, if you set up a Plan B before you have got your Plan A going, then you have effectively made the Plan B your Plan A. You must believe that you have the ability to succeed and then put 100% into boxing. If you don't, somewhere around the world, there is a fighter who will, and when you come up against him, he will have the edge.

Champ Assignment: Manage Your Expenses & Time

It shouldn't be difficult to invest in yourself. Most people do not invest in their future and waste it away on temporary moments. This includes both time and money.

Manage your expenses. What are the things that you spend money on that you don't need to, or could cut out? Allocate those expenses to your boxing career. Instead of buying the latest pair of footwear when you do not need it, use it for your future. When you are champ, you'll be able to buy a hundred pairs of that same thing, and you won't even blink an eye.

Manage your time. The majority of your time should be spent on progression. Cus and Mike attained the title because when everyone was spending time going to the cinema, restaurants, seeing dozens of girls, and so on, they were at home studying footage of the greatest fighters in history. Limit the amount of time on leisurely activities to one evening a week.

A true professional should spend around eight hours each day on his craft, just like with a traditional 9-5. If you are struggling to find the time because you work a day job, that is even one more reason to limit leisurely activities. Start by giving the time that you currently can. If you cannot give eight hours to your craft, then start small. If you are able to give an hour and a half each day, then do that. As you progress, the amount of time that you can give to the sport will naturally increase.

You can use the early mornings and late evenings to train or learn about the boxing game. Do not stay up late watching TV. Go to sleep earlier, so you can wake up earlier and fit in a workout session. If you find yourself struggling to sleep at three a.m., just get up and go for a four-mile run and a circuit workout. Instead of laying down for hours on your bed wide awake, just train instead. The hours of work will pay off.

AFFAIRS OF THE HEART

The Rocky Road of Romance

Arguably, the most impressive match of Mike Tyson's career was his ninety-one-second demolition of the then-lineal champion Michael Spinks. Part of what made it so remarkable was the fact that he could perform at such a high level, despite the problems going on in his life at the time. Before the bout, Mike's life was littered with issues and disputes. Specifically, his destructive marriage at the time was a source of extreme stress.

Media journalists back then were continually reporting the fights that he and Robin Givens were having. Before the fight with Spinks, one of the arguments between the married pair ended with cops being called to the scene after a furious Robin Givens crashed their Bentley into a car in front of them. To calm the other driver, who was yelling at the time, Mike handed him twenty-thousand dollars on the spot. With all the drama that was taking place at the time, it was a miracle that Mike was able to take care of business in the manner that he did.

As the trainer of Rocky Balboa says in the Rocky movies, 'Women weaken legs'. Regardless of whether you are a man or a woman, however, your romantic partner of choice or the sexual activities you get up to, can have an extreme effect on your abilities. Mike Tyson's first loss came in 1990, fighting in Tokyo. He later said that, leading up to the bout, he was sleeping around with the

Japanese women so much that it could be compared to 'eating grapes'. Even up until the day before the fight, he slept with four women at his hotel. It did him no good, as he ended up losing that fight. The closer you are to battle, the more your energy should be conserved so it can be used for the task ahead.

However, the real impact isn't on your physical body, as much as it is on your mind. As we have explored, the people around you can have a profound effect on your ambition, but this is especially the case with your partner because the mind is naturally more receptive. We want to open up to the person we are with. So it is essential to assess the potential of a new partner based on their ability to support your goals and adjust to your lifestyle as you progress in your career.

As for sexual activity, the old-timers of the sport have perpetuated the belief that having sex thirty days before a fight should be forbidden if the fighter does not want to be fatigued. The truth is, there is little scientific evidence to say whether this is true definitively. Although, you increase the risk of it affecting you, the closer the time of the fight comes. Everyone's physiology is different so it will differ from person to person.

Choose the Right 'Robin' Based on 'Needs'

When choosing the right partner, you must understand that this decision can have a very significant effect on your career. Relationships influence the mind heavily, whether it be for the good or the bad. A good relationship can help you ascend, while a bad one will increase the likelihood that you descend. If you make someone your partner, they must be supportive of your vision. Also, their existence cannot limit your ability to attain your goals if you believe that your career goals are a priority in your life.

However, it is also essential to understand that a relationship is a negotiation of 'needs'. Each person is there to fulfil the needs of the other, and by being together both parties agree to satisfy those needs. When a person's needs are not being met, he or she will become unhappy in the relationship, and there will be friction. Battles will occur to make sure that the negotiation is adjusted to fulfil their needs.

Therefore, you must quickly assess the needs of the other person. If you believe that you can meet these needs, while giving enough time to your craft, then you will be able to keep that person happy while you provide adequate time to boxing. Do this, and their presence will not limit you in any way.

There are three points to consider in a relationship if you wish to choose and keep the right person, and not have it negatively affect your career goals:

- **Time**. A vital need to consider for each party is time. Training for greatness requires a massive amount of time. You must dedicate a high percentage of your life to boxing each day for years. You must assess the amount of time that the other person requires to have that need met. Many champions go away for long training camps for weeks at a time, and the other person must understand this.

One thing you can do is bring the person into your world. Let your partner sit in on training sessions, or have them join you on recovery sessions. The strong exception to this is that when intense focus is required, the other person should never interfere. For example, in the last few weeks leading up to a fight, you must be fully immersed in the sport. Your mind must not be soft when a match is approaching; it must be sharp and deadly. It must be ready for war.

- **Energy and emotions**. In addition to time, energy and emotions are also needs that you have to consider. Time itself doesn't mean much if the person is not receiving your energy - but there is only so much energy we have to give in a day. Training for boxing will undoubtedly require a lot of energy and emotions. It is crucial that your partner knows that at certain moments your emotional state will fluctuate, and your energy levels will differ, like after a gym session or when you are managing your weight.

- **Understanding**. It is incredibly essential for you to share your mind with the other person. Your partner cannot be left outside of the vision. If he or she is supportive, then this person should be the first to see what you see, because he or she will be excited about helping you on your journey. Your partner must feel as if s/he is on the mission with you. This will help the person to understand the choices you make in your career and it will even help them to give good suggestions from an informed stance.

Make Your Partner Feel like S/He Is in Your Corner

The goal is to make sure that when you win, your partner feels as if s/he wins too. If you make it, so will s/he; so your partner should want to invest in making it happen. Doing this will make your goals into your partner's goals too. You must share the same purpose, and it will be in your partner's favour to never limit you.

On the other hand, if this person loses out (for example, by not having his/her needs met) when you are winning, then no matter how much s/he loves you, this person will not be in favour of you doing well. Your partner will subtly attack your ambition, because, although the win has value to you, it doesn't have value to them.

It makes more sense to build your success first before getting into a relationship. Or at least get the structure of your life in place first. However, if you do choose to select someone, it is imperative that you take care of your partner and satisfy this person's needs. If you do not, you violate the champion's trait of taking care of those around him. Even further, you will have someone close to you that does not support you, which could be destructive to the strength of your mental state.

'Don't quit. Suffer now and live the rest of your life as a champion.'

Muhammad Ali, 'The Greatest'

EVERY FIGHTER STRUGGLES

Floyd Mayweather & the Failure that Made a Winner

Floyd Mayweather Jr (50-0, 27KO) is undoubtedly the greatest fighter of the twenty-first century. From beating his long-term nemesis Manny Pacquiao to the cash cow before him Oscar De La Hoya and from the legendary Miguel Cotto to the Mexican warrior Canelo, the list on his resume is an extraordinary one.

With a historical boxing record that reads fifty wins with zero defeats, Mayweather is a symbol of victory. When he was asked about his talents, you wouldn't have to wait too long before hearing him say that 'no fighter on planet Earth can beat me; I'm the best fighter in the sport of boxing'.

His tremendous belief is what helped him to keep losses at bay throughout his professional career. However, that tremendous run of endless wins was initially ignited from a shocking loss right before he launched that career. At 19 years old, Mayweather Jr was a boxing participant of the 1996 Olympics held in Atlanta. He was the favourite to win the gold medal going into the games.

The young prodigy boxed magnificently, steamrolling through competitive fighters to get to the semi-finals of the featherweight division. On route, he even defeated a tough Cuban named Lorenzo Aragon, becoming the first American in two decades to defeat a Cuban fighter.

However, his run came to a shuddering halt against the Bulgarian Serafim Todorov. After punching the Bulgarian left, right, and centre, it seemed to most that Mayweather had definitely won the bout. So many were confused when Floyd was not named the victor. In fact, even the referee mistakenly lifted Mayweather's hand, expecting that he must be the winner.

Floyd's Olympic coach held back no verbal punches, stating that 'they need to get rid of the whole establishment' at the time. The American team tried to appeal the decision, but there was nothing that could be done; Floyd was a bronze medallist. To this day, Floyd says that he didn't win the bronze, but that he 'received a bronze. Because you can't win something if you lost'. Even though he felt that he had deserved to go through to the final, Floyd was forced to accept the decision.

A dejected Floyd wasted little time to turn professional, saying, 'we all know I got robbed … it's time for me to turn professional now; I can't deal with this amateur boxing anymore'. Many people isolate Floyd's rewards and discredit the adversity he has had to overcome to get those rewards.

Counterintuitively, it was the loss at the Olympics that pushed Floyd 'to work that much harder', because he didn't want to experience losing again. He was forced to step up his game to make sure history never repeats itself. Every fighter has to deal with their own adversities. The way in which you respond to it will define the rest of your career. Will you shy away or will you shine?

Fight Through 'The Struggle'

When we mention 'The Struggle', we are talking about all of the setbacks, challenges, and obstacles you will face on the way to reaching your goals. It is what separates the challengers from the champions and the good from the greats.

'The Struggle' will demand of every fighter that they give up and settle for less. The pressure that The Struggle puts on the fighter will be immense for many fighters, but those who are solely focused on having success by any means necessary will pass its test. They will keep fighting to reach their dream, no matter how high the pressure gets. Then by finding a way to endure and decode their personal struggles, they will be rewarded for it.

The good thing about The Struggle is that it is fair. In some way or another, every fighter who ever lived was faced with their own stack of setbacks. Struggling on the way to greatness is guaranteed. We forget this because we see champions on TV living such a glorious life. We assume that they got to the top solely with talent and no problems.

However, this impression is only the tip of the iceberg that we see. Below the water, the other side of the gigantic iceberg of pain is out of sight. The amount of success you attract is directly proportionate to the amount of struggle you are able to overcome. Look at your personal challenges as an opportunity to move up the ladder and prove to the world that you are as great as you claim.

TOUGH TIMES DON'T LAST, TOUGHT FIGHTERS DO

The Lack vs The Struggle

The reason fighters hate The Struggle is because it means having to go through pain and discomfort. No fighter wants this, and it is why they run from it. As a consequence, they will never get the rewards that await on the other side.

There are two responses that a fighter could have when facing a challenge. You will either run away, or you will endure the pain if you think the reward is worth it. If it is, this is because you view boxing as something that helps you to fill something missing in your life. This hole, or 'lacking' in your life is what the sport satisfies for you.

For example, growing up, Floyd Mayweather came from nothing. As he put it, 'we were seven deep in one-bedroom, and sometimes we didn't have electricity.' Floyd's mother was addicted to drugs in his younger days, and his father, Floyd Mayweather Sr, would sell drugs. The family house was toxic at the time of Floyd's childhood. On one occasion, Floyd Sr was shot at while he was holding baby Floyd Jr.

By no means did Floyd Mayweather Jr have it easy, but fighting was the means through which he could change not only his entire life, but his family's too. Boxing gave him the chance to fill this gap.

There are many types of gaps that boxing could help satisfy. Another example could be emotional lack. The former five-weight world champion Sugar Ray Leonard didn't suffer from extreme poverty. However, Ray's personal 'lack' in life was his social awkwardness and need for expression, and the ring provided him the place to express his character.

When this type of fighter is in the gym, he feels that he belongs somewhere and that the ring is the only place where he feels like he has any importance. Fighters may not be able to fill this 'lack' outside of the ring, which is why they fall in love with the sport.

If this is the case, it will be easier for you to go through any struggles, because the sport offers you something back in return. Every champion in boxing history used the sport to fill a lack in their life. It is part of the drive that motivates them. This is why you have to use your pain, rather than try to hide it.

Champ Assignment: What Is Your Gap?

Sit down and take a moment to define what void boxing helps you to fill. Doing this provides the perfect platform for you to build your mental endurance to fight through The Struggle. Allow your career motivation to be defined by this life's gap.

It will help you to make decisions that are crucial to your career. As long as your decisions are in alignment with satisfying this gap, you are moving closer to the life that you want. When in doubt, always make the decision that satisfies your long-term goal, even if it means sacrificing the short-term one.

Know How to Surpass Future Challenges

In the latter stages of Floyd Mayweather Jr's career, each opponent he took on presented a legitimate threat to him on paper. Before each fight, reporters would often ask Floyd Mayweather if he fears what the new opponent will bring to the table. And each time, the champion would reply, 'I've faced tough competitors in the past; I've been here before, and I know what it takes when it's a fight of this magnitude.'

Generally, the best affirmations (in the long term) are the results you get and this includes your past wins. The best proof that you are a winner is the wins in life and in the ring that you have accumulated. If you are winning your fights, then how could it be possible that you are not a winner?

Mayweather used his past experience of triumphing through great challenges to fuel his belief that he could do it again. The past victories were not in vain. With each opponent that he faced a struggle to overcome, his winning mind grew into an impenetrable fortress.

Persisting through The Struggle requires mental endurance that few boxers have. However, it is possible to build up this endurance. We build up our tolerance to the stress of challenges by going through them and learning after each one. Use those situations to practise the right way to respond correctly in the future.

If you repeatedly respond to struggles with a fearful mindset, it will become automatic. On the other hand, if you train yourself to remain calm—yet motivated—in the midst of a struggle, this will become your default response too. This is also vital for our body to learn how to respond. Not only does our mind respond in a certain way to pressure, but so does our body.

In high-pressure situations, your body will naturally release stress chemicals, leading to a rise in your heart rate when you do not feel comfortable, which, in turn, can lead to a loss of energy soon after. As you train your mind to stay relaxed, your body will catch up, and your internal state will remain stable even when you feel pressure.

Champ Affirmation:

Say this ten times when you are going through a tough situation.

'I've come through worse. I can get through this.'

Champ Assignment: Stack the Wins

When you are going through a challenge, remember that this is the most crucial time to keep going. No matter how hard it seems at the time, do not give up prematurely. There is a way to overcome it; you just need to find that way.

Once you have surpassed certain struggles, it will be easier for you to look back at the moment that you overcame it. When you are currently dealing with a new obstacle, you will naturally compare that to past challenges you have dealt with.

'Stack the wins' by accumulating numerous winning experiences not just in the ring, but also in training and in life. Although it is important to challenge yourself in training, you must also do activities in which you know you do well. This boosts your confidence. You can also practise other activities unrelated to boxing and achieve goals in other areas of your life to help foster a winning mindset.

Knowing that you navigated through past challenges, you will be confident about this new problem. If the new challenge you face isn't as intimidating as the one before, then you can easily say to yourself 'I've come through worse, so I can definitely tackle this'.

A CHAMPION'S CIRCLE

Mike Tyson: Automatic Ambition

In 1980, the aging Muhammad Ali was definitively defeated by his old sparring mate, and new champion, Larry Holmes. Mike's mentor Cus D'Amato, who was Ali's good friend and admirer, was furious. He considered Larry to be a 'bum', and an entire league, below 'The Greatest'.

The next day, Ali called Cus to talk about the fight. 'How did you let that bum beat you, Muhammad?' Cus yelled. After a few minutes, Cus told Ali, 'I have this young black kid who is going to be Heavyweight champ of the world. Make sure you tell him to listen to me.… He's almost fifteen, and he's going to be champ of the world.'

Cus gave Mike the phone, and Ali started speaking to Mike, telling him that he was sick when he lost to Holmes. 'When I get big, I'm going to get him for you,' Mike told him. And eight years later, in 1988, Mike did exactly that. Tyson demolished Holmes in four rounds to defend his title.

Having the chance to speak to one of the greatest fighters of all time undoubtedly pumped up Mike's enthusiasm to succeed. Also, as he was around Cus who was a respected boxing expert, Ali wasn't the only boxing great with whom he would speak or meet.

On another occasion, Cus had the welterweight champion Wilfredo Benitez train at the Catskill Gym, and Mike got a chance to see Benitez's championship belt. Seeing it in real life gave Mike an extra boost of desire to attain it one day. So, because of the environment Mike was put in, he was given countless experiences like this that fed his desire to capture boxing glory.

Unlike most other people his age, Mike's surroundings were focused on boxing. From meeting his idols like Benitez to being taken to watch the Olympics, despite not being a part of the team (after receiving free passes from manager Jimmy Jacobs), Mike was surrounded by a world that made it easy for him to stay focused and develop.

In his early days with Cus in Catskill, New York, it was near impossible for him to be pushed off the road to success. When other fighters from the gym went out to live their lives, Mike stayed home with Cus and devised plans for global domination. The people he met, the events he attended, the conversations he had; all aided his elevation.

A champion must intentionally adjust the world around him to reflect what he is trying to get out of it. He must fine-tune it in such a way that his ambition becomes automatic. If you want boxing success, the people, places, and activities that are a part of your everyday life must be built around this. Then, being distracted will be out of the question, and being a winner will become effortless.

Automate an Ambitious Atmosphere

Removing distractive sources is like a fighter's version of a detox. You cleanse yourself of the toxins that threaten to derail your progress. Doing nothing else, however, doesn't propel you forward; it just ensures you do not go backwards.

To move forward, replace the void with support. Specifically, seek to put a system in place that naturally encourages your progress. This means that your environmental affirmations should be shaped by a champion's mindset. Rather than resisting procrastination and trying to be disciplined, make it easier for yourself to make the right choice.

This is done by adjusting your environment so that it acts as a 'trigger' or 'cue' to make you act as the champion that you want to be. Boxing progression doesn't necessarily have to be such effort; there are already enough to deal with. It is much better that you enjoy the process with the least amount of resistance as possible.

THE SOCIAL CIRCLE

Friends & Close Associates

Look at the people closest to you if you want to measure yourself. It is said that you are the sum of the five people with whom you hang out the most. Naturally, we surround ourselves with people who are similar to us. The question is, are the people around you as ambitious as you want to be? And if you do not consider them to be ambitious, or at least positive, then are you so sure that you are different?

Find and connect with people that have an optimistic outlook in life, and it will rub off on you too. Mike himself said that he was just 'a product of someone who was on my ass all day.' Cus D'Amato was Mike's closest friend during his come up. Cus despised failure and strongly valued being a champion. So Mike did too. He became just as obsessed with the mission as Cus was.

When you are struggling or when you need to make a crucial decision, you will turn to your closest friends for advice. Positive friends will result in positive advice, and when they tell you what you do not want to hear, you can trust that it is most likely the truth. Positive confidants will push you when you start to slack off.

When Mike stayed out late and neglected training, Cus would immediately reprimand him. He would tell him to come home early and stay focused. This type of character is the only type that should be given regular permission to be a part of your inner circle.

Champ Assignment: Immersion

You must immerse yourself in the world of boxing and success. This will make it natural for you to meet people and make friends that will be favourable to your career. Make the effort to attend more boxing events, stay at the gym after workouts to help out, and visit various boxing gyms to gain more experience.

Do not immerse yourself in the wrong environments. For example, if you limit partying, it will be easier to avoid the temptation to smoke and drink excessively. Immersion in the wrong places will naturally lead to distractive activities. This is particularly important within 4 weeks of a match. Immerse yourself fully from 28 days before the fight so that your mind can start to embody a pure state of Champ-Set.

Host events (such as dinners, fundraisers, press events, or get-togethers), and invite other fighters or fight figures. Also, seek to meet ambitious people in other professions and arts, such as actors, entrepreneurs, writers, inventors, and fashion designers. Be around inspirational people, who are in love with success.

Value Takers & Givers

The people with whom you surround yourself should not just take value from you but add value too. As you begin to progress in your career, you will find that more people will start to ask for things and favours from you. The problem is that they often don't want to give anything in return.

If you give everything to the world, what is left for you? The people in your entourage must not be like this. If they do not wish to be great, this is okay; not everyone around you needs to. But, they cannot then try to infect you with any negative fake expertise either, which would be an example of taking value.

As Floyd Mayweather Jr constantly says, you must have 'a smart team' around you, who will support and help you in areas that you are not an expert. In areas where you are weak, certain people will be strong.

An example of value taking would be a team member that wants to enjoy the fruits of your hard work (e.g. free fight tickets, event invitations, lifestyle perks), but does not help you out to get those fruits (e.g. assist you in training camp, deal with career-related issues, spend time in the gym encouraging you, emotional distress). It is nothing personal, but giving too much to this type of person should be limited until you get to the point that it doesn't affect you.

Train with Talent

One of the most effective ways to quicken your progress is to surround yourself with talented people. By surrounding yourself with hard-working fighters, you make it hard to slack off, because you will fall behind everyone around you. Your standard of success will rise to a new level.

When you procrastinate, you will only need to look around you to be motivated to work hard. It is like going to the library to study as opposed to studying at home. Your procrastination will be on show to everyone. In a place that doesn't value procrastination, you won't want to be lazy.

Surrounding yourself with talented people in the fight game opens you up to new perspectives and methods of fighting. As you socialise with other fighters, you learn new tips that you would've never found out otherwise. In talent-rich environments, you will become a much better fighter, much more quickly.

Champ Assignment: The Three Talent Types to Learn from

Most people believe that the only way to learn is by getting mentored. However, that is only one method of learning; there are three. And by utilising all three, you enhance your learning rate, the amount of experience gained, and your confidence to execute what you've learnt.

The more ways you have to reinforce the skills you have learnt, the more trust you will have in your ability. The three different methods of learning include: being coached by mentors, learning with peers, and coaching your own students.

Coaches or Experienced Fighters

The first, and most common, method of learning is to be coached. In the gym, you must constantly learn from those who have more experience than you, like coaches and other fighters. Do not be arrogant and believe you are better than those who have already lived it before. What can take you weeks, or even months, to figure out, it can take someone else just minutes to teach you.

Be constantly curious. Always ask questions intending to find out what you may not know. Always assume that you know less and come from the position of wanting to open their mind up. Many coaches are flattered when someone is allowing them to express their intelligence. It makes them feel good to tell someone else what they know.

Compliment them on their knowledge and let them know you appreciate the help. By giving them the chance to feel good about what they know, you give (emotional) value to them and encourage them to keep teaching you.

When it comes to mentors, do not waste the opportunity to learn from them. It will save you from frustration, and you will be more confident going into new situations, as you will have an understanding of what works and what doesn't.

Your Peers with Similar Experience

The second method of learning comes with peers who are on the same level as you. Other fighters who are close in experience and talent to you will relate to you more than anyone else. They know what you are presently trying to do (as they are doing it too), so they relate to your current challenges the most.

For example, when you are struggling to learn a new skill, you and your peer can try to figure it out together. Unlike a coach, a fellow fighter will be able to relate to your frustration, and he will know exactly what issues you are trying to figure out.

Being able to relate to someone on this level helps you to stay enthusiastic. The good thing about peers is that they are the most inspirational example from which you could learn. If you see someone who is on your level decode a problem, this inspires you to keep trying. If our peers can do it, so can we. It heightens your willingness to learn new things. This method adds another way to reinforce new skills into your mind.

Students & Rookie Fighters

The third method of learning is to teach a fighter who has less experience than you. Coach fighters who can gain value from what you know. This is an underrated method of teaching yourself. Many fighters are unlikely to use this method, as they believe they don't gain anything out of it. It takes a selfless fighter to want to give without getting anything in return.

It may seem counterintuitive, but by teaching others, you reinforce skills into your mind in a totally new way. Teaching a rookie requires a total breakdown of the skill in a simplistic manner. As you find ways to communicate your knowledge to a student, you reinforce the basics into your own mind.

Beginners may struggle to understand you at first, but this will force you to find creative ways to get the message to them, which inevitably teaches you new (or forgotten) perspectives of looking at something.

A fighter doing all three methods will strengthen his learning and prevent boredom. When you are in a state of constant learning and also enjoying the whole process of it, you will feel on top of the world. Your belief will skyrocket as you see that you are quickly becoming better.

BUILD THE PERSONA OF A CHAMPION

Trigger Champ-Like Treatment

It can be extremely helpful if those around you see your ambition. Once they are bought into your potential, they begin to help you sustain your self-belief. After not making the Olympic team of 1984, Tyson wasn't doubtful about achieving his dreams.

Many spectators would come up to Mike and say 'you're the best', and 'you'll knock all those guys out'. Mike's spectators had become supporters who started to believe in the dream that him and Cus were crafting. It is easier to believe in your dream when you have others also believe in it and contribute to it becoming true.

In the chapter titled 'Conor McGregor: The King of Your World', we spoke about designing your vision. The next aim is to gradually get spectators to respond to you according to that vision. You can encourage this by seeding the impression of yourself as a future champion. You must project the presence of a champion. It will affect how much others will help you to bring that vision to existence.

The way people talk, act, and behave towards you on a daily basis is an environmental affirmation just as powerful as your personal affirmations. The people close to us influence our own self-beliefs. If other people assume that you are not ambitious, it will reflect in how they interact with you.

On the other hand, if they have a perception of you as someone who is great, then that will also be evident through what they say and how they act. If a hundred people think you are great and talk to you based on this belief, it will be much easier for you to believe it too.

Imagine meeting a young Mike Tyson in the amateurs. Imagine you already knew he was going to become 'Iron Mike'. How would you respond to him? When you talked to him, you would encourage him and give him pointers where you could, knowing what he would become. If you met someone new who could help him, you wouldn't hesitate to connect the two, knowing it would help him out.

Knowing what he believes about himself and what he desires in life, you would interact with him based on his beliefs. You would want to be a part of the journey in some manner if you thought it would come true. Then this would help reinforce his own self-belief. How greater would your support system be if people had the impression of you as a 'young' legend?

You must give people a great impression so they then begin to treat you like the champion you believe you are. People go off what they see and hear. Their perception of you will come from what they see and hear from you (impression), or hear about you from other people (reputation).

What do people see when they look at you? This is directly based on the image you are putting out and what it says about you. Do they see a future champion? People can only judge you based on what is handed to them. They can't see inside you, and see your dreams and aspirations, which is why you must manifest this vision.

Your Ring Persona: Win the Match Before It Begins

Your reputation isn't only received by your supporters and the people in your life. It is also a powerful component of affecting your opponent's perception of you. His perspective of you will strongly influence how he feels in training camp and how far you can get into his head when the fight comes. The degree to which you can control your opponent's emotions is the degree to which you have defeated him before the match even begins.

It's been famously said that many of Mike Tyson's opponents were defeated before the bout even began. His ring persona contributed to the mental state in which he wanted his opponents to be in. Mike Tyson's ring persona was one that was intimidating, and every aspect of his body language and the atmosphere of his fight was customised to strike fear into his rivals. He would walk confidently into the ring, often snarling at his opponents when he stepped inside of the squared circle. Even before that, his ring walk would include eerie music that suggested the devil himself was making his way to battle. Moreover, regularly knocking opponents out in spectacular fashion helped to add to the reputation that he had.

Your reputation doesn't have to be based on intimidation in the same way that Mike's was. Champions like Muhammad Ali or Floyd Mayweather had the same effect even though they were not intimidating figures. The aim is to grow your reputation and attach yourself to an aura of success so that it is difficult for your opponent to go into the match with confidence. In both your real-life and media interactions, always display supreme self-belief so that everyone else starts to accept the expectations you have set for yourself. Whether or not you are the 'A-side' or 'B-side', you will position yourself as the fighter who has more control. Naturally, you will get the results that you feel you deserve, in the ring and out.

Champ Assignment: Controlling the following factors makes a fighter 'charismatic'—the key to crafting your persona

- **Your body language.** Walk with a high chest and do not look to the floor, as that is the body language of a depressed person. Do not move showing signs of jitters, and stay assured in your movements. Have a nonchalant attitude to your posture. Be in your own world. Walk to/ in the ring with confidence, and walk in the gym as if you know you are destined for greatness. Strong confident eye contact is powerful.

- **Your workout body language.** Do you work out with confidence? Even when you tire, do not slump or look dejected. Stand upright if you can. Avoid sitting and looking down to the ground. Do not be half-hearted in your movements.

- **Your fighting body language.** Make confident body language a habit so it also becomes second nature in the ring. Opponents lose confidence when they see you cannot be discouraged. Never seem like you want out of the fight, even if you are really struggling; otherwise, it will inspire your opponent. If you are hurt or injured in the ring, look like you are ready to knock him out. If you cannot, be like Ali and exaggerate it so it looks like you are play-acting being hurt, until the pain goes.

- **Your topics of conversation.** What you talk about says a lot about you. Are you generally positive or negative? Do not speak bad about other people or be pessimistic; it gives off and creates a negative vibe.

- **The way you speak about your own boxing goals.** Do you project belief or do you show self-doubt? Do not shy away from saying you are a champion; embrace it. Describe exactly what your reign will be like. If you seem so sure of your future, people will believe there must be a legitimate reason for this.

- **Discipline.** Does your commitment mirror your affirmations? Do you show up early or late to training? Are you constantly seeking new challenges? People will judge you on how serious they think you are, based on your display of discipline. In the gym, project total focus. Whilst training, do not converse excessively and focus intensely on the workouts you are doing for the entire time that you are at the gym.

- **The tone in which you speak.** Do you sound timid and afraid, or is your voice confident and assured? Practise speaking with strong, lowered bass in your voice tone. Watch champions like Muhammad Ali or Floyd Mayweather and study voice projection. Watch pre-fight and post-fight interviews of charismatic fighters.

- **Watched or watcher?** Do you watch other people more than being the interesting person that everyone else watches? Be bold enough to have fun, be yourself, and bring other people into your world. Be a unique spectacle at some times and a dose of fun at other times.

- **Value**. Be the guy who gives out value to everyone else. Only the most successful people have the empathy to do this. Make other fighters and coaches feel good. Give out tips, entertain and always uplift those you speak to.

- **Social Media**. Display yourself in an intriguing way. Establish your personal brand and what you represent. You do not have to show off or be flashy if that is not you. Your attitude and your story are more important in connecting people to you on social media. This tells them who you are deep down. Let the people see the real you. This is what takes a boxer from being an uninteresting athlete to the interesting superstar that casual fans will pay to watch.

People buy into your own belief. It is vital that coaches, fighters, and fight fans see your vision, so they are encouraged to respond to you according to that vision. This makes it easier for you to gather evidence that the perception you have of yourself is true. The world will be reaffirming it for you, and the positive cycle of belief will gain momentum. You will then be able to take action based on those reinforced beliefs of yourself. The progress you make in life will be directly linked to the support system you have created. You will make your ambition automatic.

Champ Affirmation – The Aura of the Champion:

'I walk and talk like a champion'. Repeat it 10 times each time at various of moments of the day as you go about your business. It is particularly useful when you are doing your ring walk or in situations where you are feeling social pressure that pushes you to abandon your display of confidence.

This affirmation is effective because it reminds your mind that you are indeed a powerful champion. It allows you to feel comfortable when you are projecting yourself to the world as a strong leader.

GRIND WITH WHAT YOU HAVE

Joe Frazier's Hook from Hell, Born from Acceptance

In 1971, the Heavyweight champion Joe Frazier (32-4-1, 27KO) clashed with Muhammad Ali in what was titled as 'The Fight Of The Century'. Ali was attempting to regain his title after being stripped four years earlier and was going into the bout with no losses to his thirty-one wins.

Frazier too was undefeated, with twenty-six wins and zero losses. On the night, it was the winning run of 'The Greatest' that came to a crushing end. After a left hook from hell crashed onto the side of his pretty jaw, Ali was placed on the seat of his boxing trunks in the fifteenth round.

Ali survived that homicidal knockdown to finish the fight. However, he lost via a unanimous decision in honourable fashion, considering that any other Heavyweight in the world wouldn't have survived such a punch.

After failing to take Joe's heavyweight strap, Ali was talking to media reporters with his swollen right cheek appearing as if he was a squirrel attempting to hide a dozen acorns in it. Frazier had knocked down a couple-dozen world-class fighters with that very same left hand, and it became the most memorable weapon in the arsenal of "Smokin' Joe".

However, that famous left hook arguably formed only as a result of Joe Frazier taking advantage of circumstances that other fighters would complain about. Firstly, Joe Frazier was one of the shortest Heavyweight champions in history, standing approximately at only 5'11''(180 cm). Instead of perceiving his height as something to dwell on, he simply accounted for it and made it his advantage.

Joe fought in his famous Bobbin' And Weavin' style, coming in whilst moving his head so that he could get close enough to fire that left hook. Many fighters make the mistake of fighting against circumstances that cannot be changed. Instead, a champion must fight with what he has been blessed and make it an advantage.

Even further, Frazier's left hook may have developed partially because of an accident that happened in his younger years. On the fields of his childhood town, Joe Frazier was brazenly teasing a boar hog for his afternoon amusement with a wooden stick. Little did he know that someone had forgotten to lock the gate to the pigpen, so the angered animal was able to chase him. As he rushed to retreat, Frazier accidentally fell and split his left arm on a brick.

With not enough money to pay a doctor to tend to his torn-up arm, it was left to heal on its own. Inevitably, it never became as good as new. Frazier would later say that he was never able to fully straighten his left arm again, and it was left crooked with a lack of full motion. Interestingly, this encouraged Frazier to throw the hook more often, as it was naturally cocked to be thrown at an angle.

One of the most punishing punches in boxing history came from one of the most unfortunate incidents. Resisting this reality may have robbed Frazier of his most devastating punch. Most fighters would still try to fight it and force themselves to extend the left in a straight angle, as most fighters do. By accepting the circumstance, however, Frazier made an advantage out of what most fighters would consider to be an annoying disadvantage.

Live Life on Life's Terms

As Mike Tyson said, 'we have to live life on life's terms' and not the terms that we preferably want. If you wish to be successful, you must quickly learn to accept the things that you cannot control. A fighter cannot waste time dwelling on what he can't change, and he can't waste energy trying to reverse something just because he doesn't like it.

You must simply accept it and become aware that it is part of your journey. The solution is to make the circumstances either fit into your career safely or find the way to make it work in your favour. Go with the flow of life and move forward with the current. Don't try to swim against it.

The right way to hustle hard means *no* dwelling. It cannot be stressed enough how important it is to stay active every single day. Dwelling is the enemy of progress; it stops you from progressing daily. If a circumstance cannot be changed, dwelling will not help. With speed, focus on the things that you *can* practically improve.

In the following, we will look at some of the things you must accept along the journey to greatness, as you go from being a beginner to advanced.

THE PROCESS OF MASTERY

What Beginners Must Accept: It's Harder Than You Think

At the beginning of your boxing journey, you are a rookie to the sport. You walk into the gym excited. You feel motivated to kick some ass, just like your favourite fighter does. How hard can it be?

They make it look so easy on TV. So you're sure it'll be a breeze. Plus, you're pretty good at street-fighting anyway, and you can get the better of people when you play-fight. Boxing must be the same, right?

Wrong.

Contrary to popular opinion, boxing isn't about the strongest man; it's about the most skilful and experienced. So when the beginner steps up to the heavy bag, he quickly finds out that it is way more tiring than it looks. When he steps in the ring to spar for the first few times, he quickly learns that it isn't as easy as the TV makes it.

A beginner must accept that learning a new skill will be much harder than he ever imagined. Accepting this truth will maintain your belief that you can eventually increase your skills. The first time you spar will expel any arrogant preconceived thoughts you had about how simple it is to beat somebody up.

Some beginners will tell themselves it is hard because they don't have the natural talent. This is not the case. It is simply hard because you're new. So you must keep going until you uncover that talent. This knowledge will keep you motivated to advance to the next level.

What Intermediate Fighters Must Accept: Time & Patience

Intermediate fighters are the boxers that have a decent understanding of the sport's fundamentals. An intermediate fighter ranges from a fairly experienced amateur to a still-fresh professional fighter. The intermediate fighter has surpassed the frustration learning a new skill. Now he has to accept that the journey will take longer than he expects. Patience is what you need.

Imagine going up a mountain. It may be a struggle to get up to the first peak. And once there, you may have to continue the hike at the same height until you reach the next climb. You may even have to go down a slight dip in the terrain before you go back up to the next level. This is like your progress in your career.

You may have high moments and, at many other times, you will stall. That is okay. You have to be patient through tough times and outlast any interruptions. Accept that you have to push through to get to the advanced stage. Patience is your payment to the process.

What Advanced Fighters Must Accept: You Don't Know It All

The advanced fighter has gained experience over a number of years, giving him more skills than his peers. This is usually a fighter who has high expectations of becoming a master in the sport. An advanced fighter may be a young prodigy amongst the amateurs or experienced talent in the professional ranks.

An advanced fighter has had to be patient to get to where he is now. However, his Achilles heel is his talent. When you become really talented, your mind will start to tell you that you do not need to stay disciplined. This is typical in a sport where ego and machismo is common. However, having an ego will stop you from progressing. At this point, you need to accept that despite all of what you know, you don't know it all.

It is vital to keep testing new techniques and methods of training and fighting, as this maintains your progress. Advanced fighters with an ego do not like to experience failure, which is why they stop testing. You must always seek out feedback, whether it is good or bad, and you must be willing to struggle to learn new methods. This explains why some fighters fall off after years of dominance. They stop pushing the boundaries and do not stay on top of their game.

You must continuously reinvent yourself to adapt to the times; otherwise, you will start to fall behind. Use the 'positivity sandwich' method to criticise yourself and maintain to learn more. No fighter is perfect, and every single boxer is beatable. If a fighter has never lost, it is simply because he hasn't come up against someone who is better than him on the day.

Never get complacent and be willing to keep growing. What worked before may not work in the future. If you are good but haven't noticed improvements in a long time, you need to sit down and consider what you could work on to start seeing improvements. You may not want to do it, but it is something you have to do.

The KILLER INSTINCT

Manny Pacquiao: Be Hungry for Success Opportunities

It is the general public's belief that combat champions are brutal savages, simply fuelled by anger. They believe that anger is what drives a fighter to find comfort in hurting the man pitted against him. Admittedly, they are right about the brutal reality of what goes on inside the ring. A fighter risks his health every time he enters the ring, but what they are wrong about is the drive that pushes them from outside of it. It isn't anger but hunger that drives a fighter to reach for the top. A fighter must take this bloody trade seriously, and his hunger defines the attitude he has towards the sport.

In 2001, Lehlo Ledwaba, the 122-pound world champion was set to defend his title against Enrique Sanchez. Meanwhile, Manny Pacquiao (60-7-2), who had previously held the world title as a flyweight and was still yet to make his American debut, was settling into his partnership with his new trainer, Freddie Roach.

Ledwaba was known as one of the best junior featherweights in the division and was at the peak of his career. Two weeks before his defence, Sanchez withdrew from the contest, citing an injury. This gave the boxing association the undesirable task of having to find another world-title challenger on two weeks' notice.

Hungry for success, Pacquiao was a trainer's dream in the gym at that time. He was always working and was often described as the hardest worker you'd ever see, according to his coach Freddie Roach. Although the fight was only two weeks away, and Pacquiao had not planned for any fight, he was prepared for the opportunity to fight Ledwaba. The fight went ahead.

Pacquiao announced himself to the American public with a six-round demolition of the champion. The determined attitude he displayed at that time would later prove to be the blueprint for his career, as he went on to capture multiple titles when the odds were stacked against him in the exact same way.

The Influence of Attitude

What allowed Pacquiao to be prepared for his opportunity with Ledwaba was his serious attitude. This was no part-time job of his; it was the job that would change his life—and your approach should reflect this attitude.

There is a difference between the attitude of a regular fighter and that of a legendary champion. Your attitude strongly affects the way that you approach training. Are you optimistic and positive with a serious attitude, or are you pessimistic and negative with a passive attitude?

Of course, you need to be optimistic because this dictates how intensely you will attack your goals. A champion's compass is strongly determined by his attitude. Understand that your attitude will affect your ability to seize opportunities.

Optimism & Pessimism

Optimism and pessimism are traits that differentiate the boxer who believes that he is a winner from the one who thinks he is a loser. A winner will be generally optimistic. It will not be difficult to convince him that the outcome of something he is involved in will be a good one. Optimism is what allowed Pacquiao to take the Ledwaba fight on such short notice; many wouldn't have.

Optimism is important because the fighter will look at things with the glass half full, instead of half empty. Optimists will be good at positively reframing situations, which is how they pounce on opportunities when they arise.

On the other hand, a boxer can also be a pessimist. A pessimistic fighter downplays his chances to succeed. This lack of belief affects how they view their chances of success. Consequently, they get into a cycle of being pessimistic, then they go into matches with a lack of belief, they then lose because of that lack of belief, which damages their belief even more. The cycle continues.

The cycle of pessimism is usually started by a losing experience to which the fighter attaches himself. However, you must know that a loss doesn't make you a loser; your acceptance of consistently losing makes you one.

Losing consistently just means you are consistently choosing the wrong way of doing things. This can be changed by simply searching for the right way until you find it. Do not do the exact same thing a hundred times if it doesn't work. It is better to do a hundred different things once until you find the way that does work. Learn through experience.

Alternatively, find the right way from a mentor. Do not listen to negative fake experts who help you to sustain pessimism. As long as you are optimistic about there being a successful way, you will have the heart to find it.

OPTIMISM & OPPORTUNITY

Make Your Own Luck

An optimistic fighter has the ability to create and capitalise on opportunities that come by. Every memorable fighter had crucial moments in which he had to make the right decision. This decision could come in the form of a tactical career move or deciding to risk it in the ring for a late round knockout. Whatever that decision may be, only the optimist will be able to take risks.

A champion-in-training must reframe sticky scenarios into blessing-in-disguises. Nothing good comes from the alternative. The problem with many fighters is that they like to dwell and complain. As Floyd Mayweather Jr says, 'don't cry; don't complain; just work'. If you do not have something, don't complain about not having it. Instead, ask yourself how you can get it.

A champion must not complain about something before he has tried to do something about it. For example, Pacquiao moved to LA in 2001 to take his career further. Beforehand, Pacquiao was already a world champion in Asia. However, there was more money and opportunity in America. Instead of complaining that there aren't high purses in the Philippines, he instead uprooted to LA; he did something about it.

Many fighters fail to realise that you can create your own luck. Instead of being envious of successful fighters, why not do something about it and join them? Consistency creates chances. If you want better 'luck', then constantly be in the position for an opportunity to come.

If you are looking for an opportunity from a powerful person in the fight game, you must connect and speak with hundreds of people until you find the person who will help. Make the effort to travel and meet the people you need to or move into areas they populate.

In this era, you are able to contact those same people via social media in a short amount of time. There is no excuse. Before you complain about something someone else was given, ask yourself what have you done to try and get it?

Take the Sport Seriously

A fighter's urgency is an important component of attitude. Far too many fighters take the time they have in a boxing career for granted. You have the best chance of success if you have a serious attitude. You will project this attitude in your training. Your aura and your performance will also share these benefits.

You will understand that there is no time to waste and will be less likely to procrastinate. There is no time to let opportunities pass you by, and there is no time to give the sport less than your absolute best.

You aren't gaining time; you are losing it. With each second that goes by, you are moving closer to the end of your career. You do not want to look back on your career with regret, thinking 'if only I had been more focused, I would have achieved more'. Many fighters have looked back in the past with regret over what could have been, rather than what was. Don't let it happen. Be committed now.

Don't go as far as you feel; go as far as you think is humanly possible. Be aware that every passing moment that you do not progress is a wasted opportunity to get closer to that dream. If you have at least a decent level of talent, then you should be able to achieve illustrious honours if you work hard. If you do not achieve it, it is because you did not put in enough effort. Don't let it come to that.

THE EFFECT OF UPBRINGING

Take note of how your upbringing can affect your attitude. Fighters from different environments grow up with contrasting experiences. Inevitably, this results in contrasting mentalities. One of the biggest things that influence a fighter's attitude is his financial class. Fighters from wealthy families will have a different attitude compared to the fighters that come from poverty. In the following, let's look at those differences.

Fighters from Poverty

The vast majority of great fighters usually come from humble beginnings. 'Poverty breeds pugilists', as they say. It must be noted that there have been fighters from richer backgrounds that have broken the mould, but as Pacquiao proves, champions are often poor before their stardom. If you are struggling financially, champions, such as Pacquiao, are proof that you can make it too.

Pacquiao himself grew up selling donuts and shining shoes on the streets of General Santos City. The two dollars he earned for his first pro fight went to his mother so that she could buy rice to feed the family. This literal hunger gave birth to a hunger for success.

The most powerful trait of poverty-stricken fighters is that they have nothing to lose, literally. Growing up with no money and no stable foundation for a decent life, they will never become worse off even if they fail in boxing. This eliminates the fear of attempting to go for it. For many poor fighters who have no education or the means to find a good job, boxing may be their only option.

For Pacquiao, succeeding in boxing wasn't a desire; it was a need. Working-class fighters are literally in desperate need of changing their life. If they do not give their all to boxing, they risk starving every day for the rest of their life. These fighters train with great urgency and intensity. Their struggle breeds necessity.

Fighters from poor backgrounds are also big dreamers. When they see the media showing the glamourous life of champions, they fall in love with the idea of that life, rather than the reality. They feel their current state of living is so bad, and they imagine that the life of superstars must be the total opposite.

The truth is that superstars have their own problems too. However, dreaming about how great a champion's life must be encourages them to visualise a reality that isn't limited by logic. They visualise greatness in a mythical perspective, and they unconsciously set an amazingly high standard for themselves, which can push them even more.

The issue is that many fighters from this background usually suffer the most from belief issues. It is difficult for poor young fighters to believe they can attain their dream. They suffer from a lack of past experiences that reaffirm to them that they're worthy of success.

They don't have many examples of success, such as successful role models around them. This means that they have no source of inspiration to draw on to support their belief. It is difficult to believe that you can be great when you have never seen success around you. Success will seem like a mythical dream that people talk about, because their environmental affirmations lack positivity.

Champ Assignment: the 24/7 Mindset

Time is more valuable than money. Stay active 24/7 and be in a continuous state of war. Think of ways to merge boxing training with your daily living. Be obsessed, no matter where you are and what you can afford. You do not need to be in an expensive gym. Parks and open gyms are good places to work out. Look at the world as your training playground.

Shadow-box when you are walking back home, at the train station, or hanging out with friends. Always have your training gear nearby. After going out for leisurely activities, jog home instead of taking the bus. Run home from the barbeque, or go to the gym straight after the party. Do sit ups, press ups, and circuit workouts while you watch a movie. Use forearm grips while you walk, as it requires little focus.

Download or stream fights to watch when you are on the train. Read a boxing book when you are in a waiting room. Listen to boxing podcasts and interviews when you are driving. Put the waterproof speakers in your bathroom and listen to Ali's motivational quotes while you shower. Write your prophecy on a weekly basis when you are in a long queue. Be creative and progress all the time.

The Middle-Class Fighter

Middle-class fighters are fighters who live comfortably with little financial struggle. This fighter has a different mentality to working-class fighters. More than the working-class fighter, the middle-class fighter will not have to struggle whilst trying to train.

This fighter rarely has to worry about where the next meal will come from. He can be free of the worries that generally affects the emotional health of working-class fighters. If this is you, do not waste this advantage.

The problem is that the character traits of the middle class are generally not aligned with a champion's mindset. An elite champion is innovative and is not afraid to break the norm to be different. However, the middle class are naturally encouraged to conform to the rules. Fighters from the middle class have to learn to shed that trait and break away from the pack. This becomes important for some fighters that need to resist the doubters around them.

For example, many parents see little reason for their kid to risk being hurt in the ring when they could get a safer job, especially if he is in a position to do so. In this situation, a middle-class fighter is more likely to struggle to resist this type of pressure. He is much more likely to care about what the people around him think, and let the social pressure influence him. This can stop you from doing what you truly want to do, and in the way you want to do it.

The other major issue for a fighter from this background is urgency. Unlike poverty-stricken fighters, middle-class fighters know that they have the means to secure another job if boxing fails. Boxers are often encouraged to 'have a Plan B'. However, the fighter that thinks he needs a Plan B, will probably need one.

As previously stated, if you wish to be number one, then you need to outwork everyone else. Putting too much energy into another endeavour and 'having a plan B' means giving another fighter the chance to outwork you. Don't let the odds be stacked in his favour.

Champ Assignment: Fully Invest What You Have

If you are in this position, invest in training gear and equipment, rather than spending too much money on the latest fashion trends and gadgets. Direct that energy to boxing. Buy extra coaching, better quality food, and spend money on self-promotion.

You are in a good position to put towards marketing yourself. Study personal branding. Create good content on social media and put money towards self-promotion with advertisements (on platforms such as Facebook, YouTube, and Instagram). This is a good way to sell tickets and reach new fans extremely quickly.

Wealthy Fighters

Wealthy fighters grow up with practically no financial struggle. They relate little to the physical hunger that the poverty-stricken fighters face. Often, sons and daughters of past elite-level fighters fall into this category. This also includes the former working- and middle-class fighters who have attained stardom and riches.

You should allow yourself to be inspired by the examples of success that are already around you. It is highly likely that you know people who hold themselves to a high standard. Allow this trait to brush off on you, and let those same standards dictate the amount of success you try to attain.

The issue is that you may not find the inner hunger to push yourself in training. Boxing is a brutal sport. The training is hard and long, with blood, sweat, and tears guaranteed. The need to change his circumstances pushes a fighter to do what is necessary in training.

Fighters from well-off backgrounds do not need to change their circumstances. So, they may not want to go through the pain and suffering, because they don't have much to gain in this respect.

Secondly, wealthy fighters are the likeliest to get complacent. Complacency will set in easier when your mind is no longer aligned with The Struggle. To combat this, find ways to humble yourself and redefine what drives you. You are in the best position to allow passion to drive you. Without the need to fight for money, you fight for pure passion.

You already have the expectation of success. This needs to be balanced out with challenging situations that keep you hungry to learn, as you chase the success to match your belief.

Champ Assignment: Travel

One advantage for this fighter is that he is more likely to have the tools that help him succeed. This includes equipment and other high-quality aids for their training. Get the best equipment to help you recover post-workout. Utilise your standing to get access to the best gyms and gear and find the best coaches in the sport.

Travel globally to gain valuable experience. Make a small list of places to go and make it happen annually. Attend famous gyms, like the Mayweather Gym and the Wild Card Gym; or bring in top-class sparring, even if you are an amateur.

These travels would even make for great content. Start a vlogging series on social media so people can keep up with your story. Could you imagine getting the entire boxing world interested in your story? You don't need to wait for television networks to do it for you. You can do it yourself. Invest heavily into advertising which will catapult your ticket sales.

THE CONCLUSION OF AUTOMATIC AMBITION

Make It Happen!

This will be short and sweet as there is not much more to say. What must happen from now is simple.

If you made it to the end, I'd like to give you an applause. Well done! Not because you managed to read a book, but because you demonstrated to the universe that you are serious about your boxing ambitions. By taking the time to read this book, you have invested effort towards being successful. You are not one of those people that expect great rewards with little or no investment.

But this investment cannot stop here. You must continue the effort if you want to attain the best rewards. Make sure you continue to speak like a champion (affirmations), and live like one too (assignments). Stay on top of your game. Commit for the next thirty days. Then once you feel your mentality change, use that to inspire you to keep applying the Champ-set principles for the following two months it will become natural. The moment you stop living like a champion is the moment you aren't a champion anymore, whether you have the belt or not.

Come back and read a chapter anytime you feel it is necessary. Take this with you to the gym or a match, and read it so you can remind yourself of your power. As time goes on, you will need to personalise the affirmations, visualisations and assignments, to fit your current life situation. Define the goal you are presently trying to achieve, make the action plan to get you there efficiently, and talk yourself up (with positive affirmations), if at any point you start to doubt yourself. That's the formula for success.

Understand that you must do more than any other fighter if you want to get results that are different to everyone else. You cannot do the same thing as everyone else and expect to get different results. This is just simple logic. You have to put in the work. There is no way out of this. But *this is* the reward. It feels good to put in work, see progress and attain results/ benefits. Keep pushing past your boundaries and watch what happens. The goals that are your 'aspirations' will turn into your 'accomplishments'.

A Thank You From Reemus; From The Heart

Among one of the quotes I live by is one from the legend Cus D'Amato. It is the statement that 'greatness isn't how great you are. It is how great others come to be because of you.' Every single day, and every moment of the day, I am consumed by the desire to help someone else avoid the frustration of trying hard to look for an answer that I can give you in moments.

Boxing is my pride and joy. I credit boxing for helping me to gain a hold of my life. When the younger version of myself was cursed with anxiety and loneliness, the boxing gym came to my aid. Reading the stories of the sport's greatest champions gave me courage. I don't want to go too far into it, but this world we live in forces you to fight the truth.

Teaching the truth of life, the truth of success, the truth of belief, and the truth of your life's purpose, is by no means a priority for the authorities. This world is not made to make champions. This world is made to break them. And although the tools to support your rise are at your disposal (if you look in the right place), the tools to keep you down are eagerly shoved in your face.

When other kids spent time playing games in the playground on school breaks, I spent my time going to the library and reading the biographies of fighters like George Foreman and Roberto Duran. I quickly noticed that anyone can apply the principles of those champions to their life.

Before I suffered a grievous injury in my own boxing career, those same principles led me to train in the company of great coaches like Freddie Roach at the wild-card gym and helped me to get featured in newspapers for winning local championships.

At the time of writing, I am still trying to recover from the injury so that my talent and knowledge won't go to waste. But whatever happens, I want to be able to spread the help that would've aided me when I was younger. And if a fighter can one day say that my work helped him on his journey, then that certainly wouldn't be a waste at all.

If you believe this content can help others out, share it with them and please leave a review on Amazon to help out.

Reemus

Join thousands of fighters and fight fans and follow the brand on social media:

Subscribe on YouTube ('Reemus Boxing') – *A media channel which includes the popular 'Art of Boxing' series, where Reemus breaks down the technical skills of boxers and boxing matches. Also included is the 'Champion's Mentality' series and the 'Art of the Champion' series where we look at the past and current boxing champions to study the traits that led to their success. Other content also includes news coverage, classic film overviews and other entertaining boxing related videos.*

Follow on Instagram ('@ReemusBoxing') – *The channel which covers the latest news. I will also post your videos if they are done well. If you'd simply like to network and introduce yourself, Instagram is the place.*

Listen to the podcast ('ChampSet') – *The Champ-Set podcast is specifically for fighters who want to dive deeper into what champions do to get, and sustain, their success. We go into greater detail on motivational topics and mental strategies to help you be a focused fighter that progresses quicker than everyone else.*

***Subscribe to the blog newsletter (ReemusBoxing.com)* –** *The boxing blog is focused on three categories: gym training, mental training, and history. From articles on how to throw effective combinations and what equipment to buy, to how you can manage your anxiety and what happened when Jack Johnson took on Jim Jeffries, it can be found on the blog. Subscribe to the newsletter to get updates on the brand (promotional discounts, and video alerts).*

***Collaborations & Speaking Engagements (Reemus@ReemusBoxing.com)* –** *If you'd like to contact me, I'm reachable via email. I'm open to various collaborations and creative ideas. If you are a fighter with any questions, send me a message. For gym or event invites, and business enquiries, don't hesitate to contact me.*

'The Cus D'Amato Mind' Book *– And if you'd like to read more content, purchase my other book 'The Cus D'Amato Mind'. It is based on the philosophy of Mike Tyson's mentor Cus D'Amato and details how to apply his principles.*

Printed in Great Britain
by Amazon